Working but Poor

Working but Poor

America's Contradiction

Sar A. Levitan and Isaac Shapiro

The Johns Hopkins University Press   Baltimore and London

The Johns Hopkins University Press
701 West 40th Street, Baltimore, Maryland 21211
The Johns Hopkins Press Ltd., London

Library of Congress Cataloging-in-Publication Data
Levitan, Sar A.
  Working but poor.

  Bibliography: p.
  Includes index.
  1. Income maintenance programs—United States. 2. Poor—
Employment—United States. 3. Manpower policy—United
States. 4. Wages—United States. 5. United States—Economic
conditions—1981–   . 6. United States—Social conditions—
1980–   .
I. Shapiro, Isaac, 1957–   . II. Title.
HC110.I5L468   1987   362.5′0973   87-16973
ISBN 0-8018-3583-6 (alk. paper)
ISBN 0-8018-3584-4 (pbk. : alk. paper)

The paper used in this publication meets the minimum requirements of
American National Standard for Information Sciences—Permanence of
Paper for Printed Library Materials, ANSI Z39.48-1984.

Contents

Preface

This study examines the experiences and hardships encountered by the working poor in the labor market and the federal policy responses to ameliorate their deprivation. Contrary to the widespread perception that equates poverty with indolence, some 2 million people work full time year round but live in poverty and another 7 million poor individuals work full time for part of the year or in part-time jobs. Most disturbing is that the number of working poor has been substantially higher in the 1980s than in the 1970s.

Working but Poor profiles the working poor, examines the severity of their income problems, and analyzes the nature of low-wage job markets, including the impact of high unemployment, technological developments, and international competition on the working poor. The authors scrutinize the underlying factors that contribute to the glaring contradiction of the widespread and even rising incidence of working poor in an affluent and expanding economy.

We emphasize the role and responsibility of the federal government in alleviating the problems of the working poor. Federal policies assisting the working poor have never been generous and, with the exception of the 1986 tax bill, these policies have provided even less assistance during the 1980s than in the 1970s. Recognizing that different strategies are needed to address diverse labor market pathologies and the varied needs of the working poor, the study assesses four separate though related government efforts:

Minimum-wage and tax policies that enable the working poor to attain economic self-sufficiency;

Policies that remove employment obstacles by funding basic skill and job-training programs, by guaranteeing equal employment opportunity, and by subsidizing day care. These policies both help the poor to find work and aid the employed to advance in the workplace;

Policies that help the employable but idle poor find jobs either through matching the unemployed with jobs, providing incentives to employers for hiring the poor, or funding public service jobs; and

Income assistance and in-kind benefit policies that supplement the incomes of workers whose wages do not allow them to escape poverty.

The final chapter presents recommendations for a modified federal agenda that would more vigorously assist the working poor. The proposed reforms would be implemented over several years, ultimately carrying an annual price tag of some $10 billion. Employment and training programs would account for more than half of the proposed increases. Other major added outlays would be allocated to welfare reform and to the alleviation of the critical housing shortage for low-income families. Though the recommended outlays are considerable, we believe that the price for failing to help the working poor escape poverty may be even higher in the long run and that more assistance to the working poor is consistent with the principles of an affluent and just society which promotes economic opportunities.

Numerous individuals have been helpful to this project. Gordon Fisher, Health and Human Services, and Gordon Green and Jack McNeil of the Bureau of the Census reviewed sections of *Working but Poor*. They supplied unpublished data and helpful comments, but should not be identified with normative judgments and recommendations. Frank Gallo contributed insightful comments. We are also indebted to Barbara Webster and Jean B. Toll for their editorial contributions and Ellen Gilmore, who prepared the volume for publication.

The study was supported by an ongoing grant from the Ford Foundation to the Center for Social Policy Studies of the George Washington University. In line with the Foundation's practice, responsibility for the contents of the study was left with the center director.

1

The Concurrence of Work and Poverty

1. The Working Poor in an Affluent Nation

The working poor remain America's glaring contradiction. The ongoing concurrence of work and poverty runs contrary to the American ethos that sustained labor leads to material advancement and it negates prevailing images of poverty emphasizing deviant behavior, particularly a lack of commitment to work.

The working poor are not an isolated few. In 1985, 2 million adults—50 percent more than in 1978—worked full time throughout the year, yet they and their families remained in poverty. Another 7.1 million poor worked either in full-time jobs for part of the year or in part-time jobs. Because of limited job opportunities, inadequate skills, and the low wages prevailing in some occupations or geographic areas, they continue to have low earnings. The vast majority of the impoverished who do not work are children, the disabled, or elderly persons who can do little to enhance their income.

The American economic and political system has led to widespread economic progress providing ample opportunities for upward mobility. Throughout this century millions have moved out of poverty into the middle and upper classes, and the number of working poor continued to decline until the 1970s. Individuals who fail to apply themselves are more likely to be impoverished, and poverty can breed antisocial and criminal behavior. Greater commitment to work and skill training can rightly be expected among some of the poor. But blind faith in the free market system and a blanket indictment of the behavioral patterns of the poor are unwarranted; the difficult living conditions of the working poor and the complex factors that account for their high numbers should not be ignored. Federal government intervention is essential to improve the lives and prospects of the working poor.

The Problem

After a sharp decline in the number of working poor in the late 1960s, the level, though fluctuating with economic conditions, remained relatively stable until 1978, before rising sharply from 1979 to 1983 (Figure 1). The economic recovery since 1983 has only slightly reduced the poverty population.

A majority of the working poor are white (as are a majority of all individuals in poverty). Most of the poor who work full time year round are males; females constitute a majority of the poor who work full time for part of the year or who work part time. Although

Figure 1. The number of working poor has been higher in the 1980s than in the 1970s.

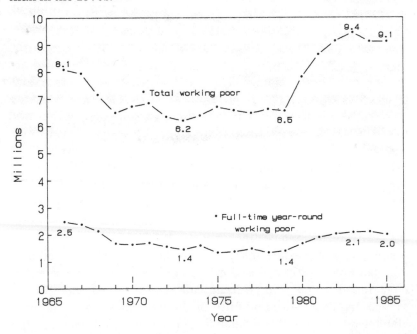

Source: U.S. Bureau of the Census

the working poor have a better chance of escaping poverty than the nonworking poor, their income and employment problems are often enduring, in part because they tend to possess limited salable skills.

To visualize the deprivation of the poor, imagine what it would be like to live on income equal to the poverty line. In 1986 the poverty threshold for a family of three was $8,738. The setting of the poverty threshold assumes that one-third of income is spent on food; in 1986 this fraction was equivalent to 89 cents per meal per person. Many working poor families have incomes well below the poverty line; they find it even tougher to meet their basic food, shelter, and medical needs. The financial difficulties of many middle-income families earning two or three times the poverty line is additional reminder of the meager basic needs that can be purchased by the poor.

In a nation as affluent as the United States, the existence of a large group of working poor is disturbing. It raises serious questions about the fairness of the rules that regulate the distribution of economic rewards. It challenges our faith in the American Dream: those who work hard will advance. It is difficult and, indeed, inaccurate to believe in this dream when millions who do work remain in poverty. Many of these jobs are dead end; they are not a steppingstone to opportunity or a better life.

When work brings low material rewards and upward mobility is unattainable, commitment to work is easily undermined and individuals so affected are alienated from the social mainstream. There is clearly a need to reconsider the impact of market wages and welfare upon incentives to work and the role of welfare in this rewards system. The current welfare policy discussion, however, places undue emphasis on the work disincentives of welfare, ignoring the limited incentives that labor bestows upon the working poor.

An economic system best promotes the work ethic when labor is sufficiently rewarded. Public policy should not only assist welfare recipients to attain economic self-sufficiency but also aid those who work but do not escape poverty. Government policies that help bring workers and their families out of poverty not only benefit the individuals directly affected, they also send a message to other impoverished adults and their children to the effect that work *does* provide a route out of poverty. A society that glorifies the work ethic should also stand ready to reward those who practice it.

The lessons to be drawn from an analysis of the working poor apply to a much larger group of workers. Millions of individuals work in low-wage jobs but have other sources of income which lift them above the poverty threshold. In 1985 almost one out of ten workers employed full-time, year round did not earn enough to raise a family of three above the poverty threshold. These low-wage workers will also benefit from rising wages and other federal policies targeted to the working poor.

The Job Market for Low-Wage Workers

The number of working poor is a reflection of economic and demographic trends, individual behavioral patterns, and the effectiveness of government policies. The unemployment rate in the 1980s has exceeded the rate in every decade since the Great Depression. In loose labor markets, low-wage workers are bound to have a difficult time. Not only are they more likely to be forced into unemployment or part-time work, but their already low wages are likely to stagnate. Chances for upward mobility, through raises or new jobs, are reduced. Increasing international competition has also contributed to a weak demand for workers, causing job losses and wage cutbacks. Federal economic policies have not addressed either problem effectively. Macroeconomic policy has focused on lowering inflation, at the cost of slack labor markets, and the government has taken only limited action to reduce the trade deficit.

Pockets of economic dislocation, moreover, are insulated from national economic growth. The working poor tend to be concentrated in troubled local economies and in a few occupations and industries, including agriculture and service employment. Many of their jobs are in the "secondary labor market" which is characterized by high turnover, arbitrary work rules, limited training, and little opportunity for upward mobility. Secondary labor market workers usually lack clout in the labor market and are heavily dependent on government policies for improvement in their employment conditions.

The number of working poor also reflects population trends. A large supply of workers in the low-wage job market can slow wage growth. Immigrants, particularly those who are undocumented, often labor in difficult situations because they are in no position to challenge inadequate wages and other working conditions imposed by employers. In the 1960s and 1970s more immigrants, women, and young workers entered the labor market, but because the economy was expanding at a healthy rate, these workers were absorbed and the number of working poor declined or, in some years, remained stable. In the 1980s, population trends were mixed: immigrants, both legal and illegal, and women continued to enter the work force in large numbers, but the number of youth entrants declined sharply. Overall, however, the labor force continued to expand and the number of working poor rose.

Federal Policies

In addition to broad macroeconomic and trade policies, the federal government influences the fate of the working poor with a wide variety of more targeted policies. These policies specifically affect worker compensation and help break down skill and other barriers to employment. They also help the poor secure employment and supplement their income through welfare and social insurance.

The federal minimum-wage and tax policies have a direct impact on the compensation of low-wage employees. The minimum wage acts as a floor under wages which helps to ensure a minimally acceptable standard of living. Established in 1938, the minimum wage was generally strengthened until the 1980s—both in terms of coverage and in level of support.

The support level of the federal minimum wage has fallen dramatically in recent years, reducing the earnings of millions of workers, many of whom are poor. In 1987 the purchasing power of the minimum wage was at its lowest level in more than three decades. The earnings of a full-time year-round minimum-wage worker with two children was 23 percent short of the poverty line. In contrast, throughout most of the 1960s and 1970s, full-time work at the minimum wage lifted a family of three above the poverty threshold. Exemptions from coverage and· weak enforcement of the Fair Labor Standards Act allow employers to pay many workers less than the federal minimum, further undermining the effectiveness of the minimum-wage standard.

While the value of the minimum wage declined during the first half of the 1980s, the taxes of the working poor rose. Federal taxes for a two-parent family of four living at the poverty threshold jumped from 1.8 percent of income in 1979 to 10.4 percent in 1985. However, the 1986 tax law gave generous relief to the working poor, reducing their tax burden to the levels of the late 1970s. The tax law increased the amount of income exempt from taxes and raised the earned income tax credit which offsets social security taxes for low earners with dependents. These tax provisions are indexed to inflation and will free the working poor from onerous federal taxes for the foreseeable future.

Skill deficiencies impede gainful employment of many Americans. Approximately one in eight is illiterate; one in four lacks a high school diploma; and one in twelve has a work disability. Federal second-chance education and training programs are designed to assist those who do not acquire adequate skills through the elementary and secondary education system.

Federal second-chance programs target various categories of individuals. Basic education programs lead to high school equivalency degrees and prepare participants for vocational training, and rehabilitation programs provide training assistance to the disabled. The Job Training Partnership Act (JTPA) funds skill training for economically disadvantaged youth and adults. The Job Corps program, which is part of JTPA, provides comprehensive skill training in a residential setting for disadvantaged youth. Second-chance programs have always been underfunded relative to the number of individuals who lack salable basic skills. This disparity was exacerbated in the 1980s when Congress cut funding for employment and training efforts.

Low-wage workers with adequate skills are often prevented from moving into higher-paying jobs because of other employment barriers. Spurred by the civil and women's rights movements, federal antidiscrimination policies have opened employment opportunities to women and minorities since the mid-1960s. However, the Reagan administration's weak enforcement of antidiscrimination laws threatens continued progress in the workplace for women and minorities.

Workers with children are often prevented from securing full-

time or even part-time employment because of the lack of adequate, affordable day care. This situation is particularly true for
the rising number of single-parent families living in poverty. The
federal government either directly or indirectly subsidizes some
day care through the social services block grant program, Head
Start, and the child care tax credit. If adequate, low-cost day care
was more readily available, the work effort of the adult poor would
increase and the lives of poor children would improve. However,
during the 1980s the federal government slashed block grant funding by almost one-third even though day care facilities were available to a minority of impoverished parents, and the child care tax
credit primarily benefits middle- and upper-income families.

The federal government plays a direct role in improving the
functioning of the low-wage labor market through the federally
funded, state-administered employment service which matches
workers with job openings. When the job-matching process is expe-
dited, unemployment is reduced. The employment service helps fill
millions of jobs each year but it has been criticized for the low
quality of its job placements and for inefficiency.

The targeted jobs tax credit provides a tax credit to employers
who hire low-wage workers. The credit is intended to encourage
employers to hire workers, particularly poor youth and welfare
recipients, who because of low skills or other employment barriers have trouble breaking into the job market. Disadvantaged
youths more than any other group have been certified for the
program. Because of an inadequate verification process, however,
information is not available about the total number hired as a
result of this program. There is some evidence that the act frequently subsidizes the employment of workers who would have
been hired in any event.

The federal government has also periodically been the employer
of last resort by creating public service jobs for the unemployed.
The primary public service program of the 1970s was eliminated
in 1981, thus depriving the government of a useful policy tool
that had helped the unemployed to find jobs. Funding of smaller
public service employment programs for the elderly and summer
jobs for youth continued in the 1980s.

In sum, the funding of federal employment and training programs fell by more than half from 1981 to 1987. These cuts have

curtailed employment opportunities for the working poor. They have taken place even though funding of federal second-chance programs which promote upward mobility and economic self-sufficiency has always been meager and notwithstanding that employment programs which focus on the needs of the unemployed can prevent individuals from being destined to a life of poverty.

Federal policies that make work pay and enhance employment opportunities reduce the need to support the able-bodied poor. But in part because federal policies do not significantly promote upward mobility, millions of able-bodied individuals do require welfare as a last resort. If these workers are to escape poverty, their earnings must be supplemented by welfare.

The federal income security system is vast and includes cash assistance, in-kind benefits, and social insurance programs. Despite widespread public concern with strengthening the welfare system's work incentives, recent program cuts have had a heavy impact on the working poor. These reductions decrease the incentive to work since the loss of welfare benefits can cancel out the rewards of work.

The extent of government support provided to the working poor varies sharply. The primary means-tested cash assistance program, Aid to Families with Dependent Children, has always been of only moderate assistance to families with earnings; 1981 program changes further reduced this group's benefits. In 1983, only 6 percent of AFDC families had any earnings, compared with 13 percent four years earlier. Federal in-kind benefit programs include food stamps, medicaid, and public housing assistance. Funding for these programs is much higher than for cash assistance and they do give working poor families some relief, but only a minority of the working poor is served by each of these programs. Social insurance programs, including social security and unemployment insurance, extend benefits to recipients of all income levels. These programs provide much help to those in poverty, but not when they are working.

In 1981 Congress rejected the Reagan administration's mandatory work requirement proposal for able-bodied recipients on welfare. The resulting congressional compromise encouraged states to strengthen those programs that attempt to move welfare recipients into gainful employment. The results of these work and welfare programs have been encouraging but, if they are to be more than marginally successful, they require larger government investments in training and job creation.

The Future

Throughout much of the 1960s and the 1970s, the federal government implemented policies that provided substantial assistance to the working poor. Macroeconomic policies sought to minimize overall unemployment, and job-training and job-creation efforts were expanded. The minimum wage provided a reasonable wage floor and Congress enacted new initiatives including equal employment opportunity laws. Welfare and social insurance programs were generally strengthened. All of these factors contributed to progress in the provision of economic security.

In many of these areas, federal policy changes have recently resulted in less assistance for the working poor. Although the political climate is now more favorable to antipoverty programs than it was at the beginning of the decade, opposition to these programs remains strong, and the troublesome budget deficit makes it unlikely that the federal government will commit substantial additional resources to assisting the working poor. Moreover, current economic trends do not bode well for this group. There are few signs that the unemployment rate will drop significantly or that wage rates will rise sharply. The United States trade deficit dampens wage growth and causes job losses.

The outlook for the working poor is not completely dismal. Despite retrenchments, the policy framework for assisting the working poor has remained largely intact. Some programs in aid of the working poor can be strengthened without raising the federal deficit. Restoring the minimum wage to its traditional level, for example, will not raise federal expenditures nor will adequate enforcement of equal employment opportunity laws. Other programs, particularly training and placement policies, require larger up-front investments but in the long run some of these funds are recouped through increased tax revenues and a drop in welfare costs. Promoting gainful employment is ultimately a cost-effective investment for the federal government and society as a whole. Most important, it helps the poor achieve more attractive and rewarding lives.

The direction and benefits of federal policies for the working poor depend on the political will to design and adopt the federal policies that provide assistance. The 1986 tax legislation helped the working poor and also indicated that their problems are becoming more widely recognized. Efforts that help individuals work their way out of poverty and off of welfare offer promise as an attempt to balance the goals of economic support and economic self-sufficiency. In addition, they support the underlying premise and promise of the work ethic. The 1986 election results were an additional signal of the continued public support for the notion that the federal government should play an active role in helping the poor. The public is especially supportive of programs that promote upward economic mobility among the poor who are trying to help themselves. Policies designed to help the working poor may again become a national priority.

2

The Setting

2. Profile of the Working Poor

Most poor adults who are able to work and find jobs do so, but the number of working poor was sharply higher in the first half of the 1980s than in the 1970s. The vast majority of the full-time year-round working poor are white; two-thirds are males; more than half live in nonmetropolitan areas. The majority of the partially working poor are females. As might be expected, the working poor are more likely to have skill deficiencies than the population as a whole.

Most impoverished adults who do not work are elderly or disabled persons, full-time students, or parents of young children. Of those poor adults who head households and who do not fall into one of these categories, one-third work year round and another third work intermittently. The difference between the work experience of the poor and that of the general population is partially explained by the high proportion of the poor who cannot find jobs or are involuntarily employed in part-time positions, and, no doubt, some of the poor could find work if they were properly motivated.

The income of many working poor families is well below the poverty line, even when the value of in-kind benefits such as food stamps or medical assistance is included. The extent of their deprivation depends on how long they remain in poverty. The poverty spells of the working poor are less prolonged than the spells of those in poverty who do not work; nevertheless, many of the working poor experience long periods of economic deprivation.

The Big Picture

The working poor account for a small fraction of the employed. In 1985, only 2.7 percent of all full-time year-round workers were poor and only 7.3 percent of all those with work experience lived in poverty. Employment does enable most workers to escape poverty. In absolute numbers, however, the working poor constitute a problem of significant magnitude. In 1985 an estimated three-fifths of the poor lived in family units in which someone worked during the year. About 7.1 million individuals were counted among the partially working poor. The poor who worked full time year round numbered 2.0 million individuals including some 1.2 million heads of household. Including children and other family members, an estimated 6 million poor individuals lived in family units in which someone worked full time year round.

Earnings constitute a significant source of income for the poor. Not counting the value of in-kind benefits, earnings account for two-thirds of the income of impoverished two-parent families with children and one-third of the income of impoverished female-headed families.

From 1978 to 1985, the number of full-time year-round working poor rose by 50 percent and the number of partially working poor rose 35 percent. In contrast, the number and percentage of working poor fell sharply during the 1960s before the number essentially stabilized in the 1970s while the percentage dropped. This progress was reversed from 1979 to 1983, when the number and percentage of working poor jumped dramatically before declining slightly in the subsequent years of economic recovery (Figure 2). The economic situation and the policies of earlier years can be studied to see why they had more success in those years in addressing the problems of work and poverty.

The rise in the number of working poor parallels other trends that indicate that income distribution in the United States is recently becoming more unequal. A Congressional Research Service study found that from 1947 to 1967 family income became more equally distributed in this country but that the trend reversed thereafter.[1] In particular, the share of total family income (excluding in-kind benefits) held by the lowest population quintile has fallen. In 1979 their share was 5.2 percent; by 1985 it had dropped

Figure 2. In the 1980s the working poor have accounted for a higher proportion of all workers.

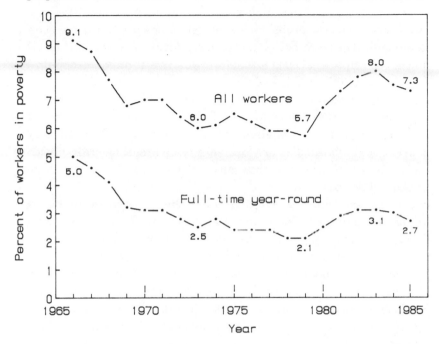

Source: U.S. Bureau of the Census

to 4.6 percent. In contrast, the comparable share of the wealthiest fifth of the population rose from 41.7 percent to 43.5 percent of total income. This uneven distribution of income suggests the need for corrective action aimed at achieving a more equitable wage system that would allow at least full-time workers to escape poverty.

Characteristics

The demographic characteristics of the working poor indicate a problem spread across population groups. However, the vast majority of the working poor are white and of prime working age. The working poor are almost equally divided between women and men, although impoverished men are more likely than poor women to be full-time year-round workers (Table 1). Child-care responsibilities often limit women to part-time work.

The working poor are highly concentrated in nonmetropolitan areas and "poverty areas" (areas in which 20 percent or more of the population were below the poverty level). Almost half of all employed impoverished household heads live in nonmetropolitan areas where only a third of all households are located. The full-time year-round working poor are even more heavily concentrated in nonmetropolitan areas; over half reside there. Some 35 percent of working poor householders live in poverty areas whereas 17 percent of all households are located in such areas. Overall growth in the United States economy may not be of much help to these pockets of poverty.

Serious skill deficiencies contribute to the employment problems of the working poor. Their education levels are less than those of the working nonpoor. It is also likely that the working poor are disproportionately represented among the estimated 13 percent of the population judged by a government study to be functionally illiterate.[2] Four percent of the full-time year-round working poor suffer from physical disabilities; proportionately twice as many of the partially working poor have physical disabilities.[3] Skill-

Table 1. Characteristics of the Working Poor, 1985

	Partially working poor	Full-time year-round working poor	All working poor
Race			
White	74.5%	79.9%	75.7%
Nonwhite	25.5	20.1	24.3
Sex			
Male	46.5	66.5	50.8
Female	53.5	33.5	49.2
Age			
21 years or less	25.4	8.1	21.6
22–59 years	69.9	86.0	73.4
60 years or more	4.7	5.9	5.0

Source: U.S. Bureau of the Census

training programs, especially those which emphasize basic competency, are essential to alleviate the problems experienced by the
working poor.

Not all the working poor have skill deficiencies. They are employed in a surprisingly wide range of occupations. Although they
are highly concentrated in service and agricultural jobs, an inde-
terminate but significant proportion of low-wage workers could
adequately fill more demanding and better-paying jobs. The problems of the working poor are due both to supply factors—unskilled
workers—and to demand factors—a lack of jobs. The lack of skills
consigns some individuals to low-wage positions whereas the un-
availability of higher-paying positions either because of discrimination or insufficient demand keeps some skilled workers in poverty.

How Much Do the Poor Work?

Poor adults do tend to work less than adults who are not poor. A
possible explanation for this fact is that the poor are indolent. An
alternative explanation is that many individuals are poor either
because they are incapable of work or they cannot find jobs that
would provide them with earnings sufficient to escape poverty. The
second explanation applies to most poor adults. The commitment to
work is strong among the poor. The majority of the adult nonworking poor are elderly or disabled persons, students, or parents of
children under six years of age. That those who claim to be are
seeking work is supported by the sharp drop of those in poverty
claiming to be unemployed in periods of economic growth.[4] In addition, the number of people seeking work far exceeds the number of
job vacancies, even during boom times.[5]

In 1985, of the 22.0 million individuals fifteen years or older who
lived in poverty, 42 percent worked at least part of the year. Only
14 percent of poor adults compared with 49 percent of the nonpoor
worked year round (Table 2). More than half of poor male adults
had some work experience during the year as compared to one-
third of female adults. Two of every five impoverished white adults
and one of three impoverished black adults also had some work
experience during the year. These differences in work effort are
explained in part by the parental responsibilities of women and by

Table 2. Numbers employed (in millions), 1985

	Nonpoor	*Poor*
Total, 15 years and over	162.0	22.0
Worked	115.3	9.1
50 to 52 weeks	79.8	3.0
Full time	70.5	2.0
49 weeks or less	35.6	6.1
Did not work	46.5	12.8
In armed forces	1.0	.1

Source: U.S. Bureau of Labor Statistics

the greater difficulty experienced by women and blacks in finding jobs.

The poor are highly represented among the ill or disabled and among those unable to find work (Figure 3). Analysts differ over acceptable explanations for not working. For example, because the majority of all women with children under six years old are currently in the labor force, some analysts hold that "keeping house" is an insufficient reason for not working. However, because adequate day care is often too costly for the poor, working full time may not be a viable alternative for a significant proportion of mothers with young children.

One study, which assumed that the disabled, the elderly, full-time students, and female-household heads with children less than six years old are adults not expected to work, found that among those poor household heads classified as expected to work, one-third worked year round and another third worked part of the year. Many of those who did not work were unable to find jobs (Figure 4).

The number of weeks worked by poor household heads has fallen over time. In 1967 over half of such individuals as compared to one-third in 1984 worked year round. The decline in weeks worked is partly explained by the doubling of the unemployment rate during this time.

In 1984, one in five impoverished families, or 1.4 million of the 7.3 million poor families, had two or more workers. This proportion is much less than the proportion of all families with multiple work-

Figure 3. The poor are more likely than the nonpoor to be ill or disabled or unable to find work.

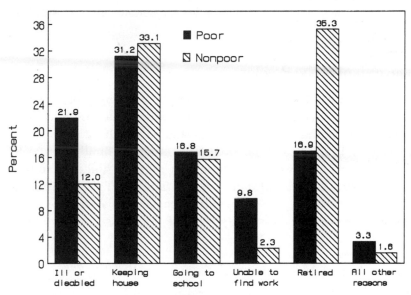

Source: U.S. Bureau of the Census

Figure 4. Most of the adult poor expected to work do work.

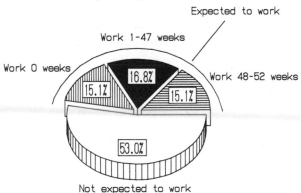

Source: Sheldon Danziger and Peter Gottschalk, *Work and Poverty: The Special Problems of the Working Poor,* Hearing before U.S. Congress, House Committee on Government Operations, December 12, 1985, p. 13.

ers (56 percent). The difference is partly due to the unemployment problems of the poor, the inability of many poor adults to work, and the greater proportion of single-headed households among families in poverty.

The Extent of the Problem

The severity of the problems faced by the working poor depends on the size of their income deficit—the difference between their family income and the poverty line—and on the duration of their poverty spells. The total money income of a poor family in which the household head works full time year round is higher than the total money income of all impoverished families. This differential disappears, however, when per capita income is considered because the average working poor family is larger than other poor families.

	All poor families	Poor families in which household head worked full time year round
Median income	$5,455	$7,118
Mean income	5,457	6,152
Per capita income	1,501	1,487

The income deficit varies depending on family circumstances, but can be substantial. In 1984, the poverty line for a family of four was $10,609, whereas poor families in which the head worked full time year round averaged 4.1 members and had a mean income of $6,152.

The above figures include only the money income of the working poor and exclude the value of in-kind benefits. The largest in-kind benefit programs for the poor are food stamps, medicaid, and public housing subsidies. These programs provide considerable assistance to the working poor. At most, however, only one in three working poor families benefit from each of these programs. In 1985, depending on the methodology used in estimating the value of the assistance received from all food, housing, and medical benefits, 12 to 24 percent of household heads in poverty who worked were lifted out of poverty by in-kind benefits.[6]

Another factor that can lead to an overstatement of the poverty problem is any unreported income of the poor. On the other hand, some analysts argue that the official poverty number is too low. The poverty line was devised in 1965 and is based on the cost of an emergency food diet multiplied by three. Because of rising prices for necessities such as housing and health care, it would be more accurate if the multiplier were larger. Raising the poverty line would considerably increase the number of working poor. In addition, the official poverty line is based on pretax income so it neglects to count those who fall below the poverty threshold because of taxes. The debate over the appropriate level of the poverty line is beyond the scope of this book. The point to be made here is that even if the value of all in-kind benefits is included, fewer than one in four working poor households escape poverty.

There is a high incidence of mobility in and out of poverty. The working poor are more likely to move off the poverty rolls than the nonworking poor; however, a sizable proportion of the working poor experience more than simply one bad year in a string of good years. To analyze the duration of poverty for the working poor requires longitudinal studies that track the employment and income status of specific families and individuals over time. One study of this nature is the University of Michigan's Panel Study on Income Dynamics (PSID).

Using data for the decade ending in 1978, the panel's researchers concluded that poverty is much more transitory than previously believed. They found that, on average, 40 percent of those in poverty in any given year escaped poverty the next year and that only 19 percent of the poverty population was "persistently" poor (individuals poor in eight of ten observation years). They used a strict definition of persistently poor, neglecting, for example, individuals who experience poverty in five out of ten years who clearly have enduring income problems. Because so many individuals move in and out of poverty, one in four of all Americans experienced poverty during the ten-year study. However, an individual or household that was poor in any given year had a much greater chance than someone who was not poor in that year of experiencing enduring income problems. The researchers found that compared to a nonpoor person an individual who was poor in one year was twenty times more likely to be poor in the succeeding year.[7]

A later analysis of the PSID data questioned these findings, persuasively suggesting that methodological flaws led the PSID researchers to undercount the length of poverty stays.[8] The more recent study concluded that many poverty spells are short, but that the majority of the poor at any given time are subject to long spells of poverty. The average poverty spell (expected consecutive years in poverty) of all those in poverty at any given time is twelve years. For first-year entrants into poverty, the expected spell during the study period is 4.2 years. The analysis elaborated on these possibly counterintuitive results with an analogy: most hospital admissions are short term, but a high proportion of the patients at any given time are long term.

These findings apply to the entire poverty population, not merely the working poor. To break down the results, the working poor have shorter poverty spells than the nonworking poor and the full-time year-round working poor have shorter spells than the part-time working poor. Those who are working or are capable of working have a much better chance of raising their income. Almost three in four poverty spells end because of an increase in earnings (as opposed to a rise in unearned income or a change in family status). The proportion is higher among male-headed families.[9] Using the panel data, researchers found that the demographic characteristics of the temporary poor (individuals in poverty one or two years out of the ten-year observation period) are similar to those of the rest of the population. Over three in five household heads in this category worked at least 1,500 hours annually (full-time year-round employment totals about 2,000 hours). Very few households headed by nonelderly white men (the households in which the full-time year-round working poor are concentrated) are persistently poor; one-third of the persistently poor population is elderly and more than four of every ten live in households headed by women.[10] One recent analysis supported the finding that persistent poverty among men is more likely among older workers. It found that 41 percent of men who worked full time but were poor in 1970 were poor or nearly poor in 1980, but that 62 percent of those who continued to have income problems were forty-five years or older as of 1970.[11]

Agriculture Department researchers found that the probability of nonmetropolitan impoverished households remaining persistently poor was also much lower among families whose head worked a significant amount. These researchers defined persistently poor persons as those who lived in impoverished families for at least three years from 1978 to 1982. Whereas 38 percent of all nonmetropolitan poor were classified as persistently poor, among impoverished families in which the household head worked 1,691 hours or more in 1981, only 12 percent were persistently poor.

Evidence of mobility among the working poor should not obscure the serious and enduring labor market and income problems that this group faces. Their prospects may be better than those of the nonworking poor, but many of the working poor have long-term earnings problems. More than any other indicator (including demographic characteristics such as education or race), the best predictor of future status in a low-wage job is whether or not a worker is currently in a low-wage job. A core group of working poor remains impoverished for many years. One study found that from 1969 to 1978 the one in twenty men who fell into the lowest-earning decile seven or more times accounted for 44 percent of all the lowest-earning decile years.[12]

Earlier studies of mobility among the working poor may not be applicable to the current working poor population. The cited studies primarily analyzed data from a period when the number of working poor was either falling or stable. In the first half of the 1980s, the unemployment rate and the number of working poor were higher than in the 1970s; moreover, in recent years, federal policy provided less assistance to the working poor. The deteriorating conditions of the 1980s may have exacerbated the labor market difficulties of the working poor and extended the duration of their poverty spells.

A Chronic and Aggravated Problem

The number of working poor has been higher in the 1980s than in the 1970s and most poor adults who do not work do so for compelling reasons. Although workers are more likely to be in poverty if they are minorities, women, or deficient in skills, most of the working poor are white, half are men, some are skilled, and they are found in a wide range of occupations. In-kind government aid lifts at most a fourth of poor workers out of poverty. The working poor have a much better chance of escaping poverty than the nonworking poor, and the full-time working poor are more likely to escape poverty than the partially working poor. Nevertheless, the income and labor market problems of the working poor are often enduring and the duration of their poverty spells may be growing longer.

3. Low-Wage Job Markets

The working poor are highly concentrated in a few low-wage occupations. These jobs offer little opportunity for upward mobility and lack the protections common in better paid and more stable occupations. Low wages are only one of the labor market problems common to the poor. Forced idleness and involuntary part-time employment are other significant problems. Many low-wage workers live in fairly affluent families, but, not surprisingly, low-wage employment is closely related to family income problems.

The recent rise in the number of low-wage workers reflects the economy's lackluster performance. High unemployment rates and foreign competition during the 1980s and low productivity growth since 1973 have contributed to stagnating wages. The rapid pace of technological change also influences the nature of the low-wage job market. A booming economy would improve conditions in the low-wage labor market, but some of the working poor are concentrated in areas and jobs that are frequently insulated from overall economic growth.

The supply of low-wage workers has been swelled by the entry into the workplace of large numbers of immigrants, women, and baby boomers. The job market has shown remarkable strength and flexibility in absorbing these workers and, to some extent, this influx has abated. Overall, however, the demand for labor has not kept pace with rising supply, indicating the need for federal intervention to address the problems of low-wage workers.

The Jobs of the Working Poor

Individuals who work full time year round yet remain impoverished are found in most occupational groups but they are disproportionately concentrated in service and agricultural occupations.
Only 8 percent of all full-time year-round workers who head households are found in service occupations—household, production,
food, health, cleaning, building, and personal services—but more
than twice that number of full-time year-round workers living in
poverty are employed in such positions. Similarly, six times as
many farm workers are impoverished than would be expected
given their numbers in the overall working population (Figure 5).

An individual's chance of being impoverished is closely related to
that person's occupation. Only 3.5 percent of all full-time year-
round workers who headed households, compared with 7.8 percent

Figure 5. The full-time year-round working poor who head households are disproportionately distributed across occupations.

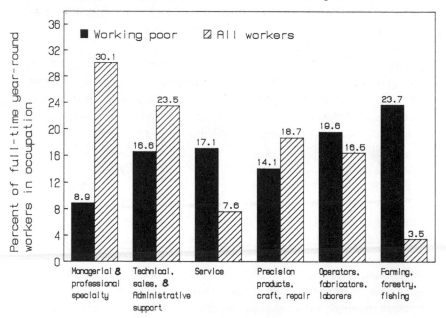

Source: U.S. Bureau of the Census

in service occupations, and 23.2 percent employed in farming, forestry, and fishing, were impoverished in 1984. Further disaggregation of occupational categories provides additional evidence that impoverished earners are heavily concentrated within specific occupations. Sixteen percent of food service workers and 31 percent of farm operators and managers worked full time year round but lived in poverty.

A surprisingly large proportion of the full-time year-round working poor are self-employed. In 1984, about 700,000 or one-third of full-time year-round impoverished workers were self-employed. An estimated one-third of these earners were farmers and one-fifth were in sales.

The occupational composition of low-wage earners varies sharply by sex. Equal numbers of men and women work full time year round and earn less than $7,000 annually. Low-earning men are more likely than low-earning women to remain in poverty because their incomes are less likely to be supplemented from other sources. Men are heavily concentrated in farming and women are heavily concentrated in sales and service occupations. The occupational distribution (in percentage) of low earners in 1983 follows, in Table 3.

The duration of poverty among household heads reinforces these data, indicating disproportional occupational distributions. A study of the poverty duration among nonmetropolitan household heads found that, among female household heads classified as persistently poor, almost two-thirds worked as service and household

Table 3. Occupational distribution of low earners, 1983

	Men	Women
Managerial and professional speciality	14.8%	11.7%
Technical, sales, and administrative support	15.9	33.8
Service occupations	12.0	35.7
Precision products, craft, and repair	13.9	2.2
Operators, fabricators, and laborers	13.4	11.7
Farming, forestry, and fishing	30.0	4.9

Source: U.S. Bureau of Labor Statistics

workers; among male household heads so classified, over half were
employed in farming.[1]

The poor who work part time are even more likely to be concentrated in trade and service industries than are the full-time working poor. More than one-third of all persons employed in service
occupations worked part time. The poor are highly represented
among part-time employees.

The occupational distribution of the working poor suggests the
need for new and varied policy solutions. The working poor are
likely to be employed in the secondary labor market in which work
is unstable and menial, discrimination is widespread, and there is
little opportunity for advancement. Federal intervention, such as
an effective minimum wage, is necessary to provide minimum adequate work conditions on such jobs. The problems of the self-
employed working poor are harder to determine because they may
have unreported income, may be experiencing a single bad year, or
may have assets that would help them during cyclical downturns.
It is also more difficult to design policies to assist the self-employed
because they are unaffected by traditional federal regulations such
as the minimum wage.

Unemployment, Part-Time Employment, Low Wages

Three labor market problems plague the poor: unemployment,
involuntary part-time employment, and employment at low wages.
These problems are interrelated. An individual can experience
both unemployment and part-time employment at low wages in
the same year. The unemployed can find part-time or full-time low-
paying jobs which will drive down the unemployment rate but
drive up the number of working poor.

Since 1982, the Bureau of Labor Statistics has examined the
labor market and poverty connection in its annual "hardship" report.[2] This linking of employment status, earnings, and family
income is critical in measuring the severity of labor market problem faced by low earners.[3] The family is an integrated spending
unit and the earnings of one family member or income from other
sources eases the hardship caused by a particular labor problem
affecting one individual in the family unit.

The BLS survey annually measures labor market hardships experienced by three groups: unemployed workers, involuntary part-time employees (part-time workers who seek full-time jobs), and full-time year-round workers who earn less than $6,700 (or less than the minimum wage of $3.35 an hour while working 40 hours a week, 50 weeks of the year). Because the BLS reports include only workers earning less than the minimum wage, this methodology understates the problems of workers with low earnings. Annual earnings of $6,700 fell $1,600 short of the poverty line for a family of three in 1984. Moreover, some workers who earned above $6,700 remained in poverty.

	Total workers (in millions)	Number in poverty (in millions)	Percentage in poverty
Persons with unemployment	21.5	4.7	21.9%
Involuntary part-time employment	14.4	2.6	18.0%
Low earners	4.5	1.4	31.1%

Some workers experience more than one kind of labor market pathology in a year. Adjusting for overlap, the total number of workers with labor market problems in 1984 was 33.7 million, including 7.1 million who lived in poor families.

Three conclusions can be drawn from these data. First, as measured by BLS hardship standards, the labor market problem affecting the largest number of individuals is unemployment. This is followed by involuntary part-time work and low earnings. Second, a majority of workers with labor market problems, including almost 70 percent of low earners, do not live in impoverished families. The workers escape poverty either because they live alone or in small families or, most important, because their income is supplemented by the income of other family members, welfare, or nonwage income. Many low earners, in fact, live in fairly well-off families. In 1984, when the poverty threshold for a family of three was $8,277 and $10,609 for a family of four, almost half of all low earners in 1984 lived in families with total income of $15,000 or more.

	Total workers	<$5,000	$5,000– 9,999	$10,000– 14,999	$15,000+
Number of low earners (millions)	4.5	0.8	1.0	0.6	2.1
Percentage distribution	100.0%	17.8%	22.2%	13.3%	46.7%

Policies that affect low-wage earners will often influence the welfare of families from a wide range of income levels.

Third, there remains a strong connection between labor market pathologies and poverty. Almost 5 million individuals who were unemployed in 1984 and 2.6 million who were involuntarily employed part time were impoverished. The connection between low earnings and poverty is direct: 31 percent of low earners were in poverty. Almost 40 percent of individuals employed full time year round who earned less than $3,000 lived in poverty compared to only 7 percent of workers who earned between $6,700 and $10,000.

	Total workers	<$3,000	$3,000– 6,699	$6,700– 9,999	$10,000+
Total (millions)	70.4	1.8	2.7	6.1	59.8
In poverty					
Number	2.1	0.7	0.7	0.4	0.3
% of total	3.0%	38.9%	25.9%	6.6%	0.5%

Federal policy options have varying effects on different labor market problems. Policies that stimulate overall economic growth will benefit the unemployed as well as part-time and low-wage workers. Similarly, raising the basic skill level of the American work force should diminish the extent of all labor market problems. Some policies, however, are more targeted. The employment service, for instance, primarily helps the unemployed, not those who have jobs. Some policies, in fact, may alleviate one of the three labor market problems while exacerbating another. The minimum wage is a good example—a high minimum wage helps the working poor but it may also reduce employment opportunities.

The Demand for Low-Wage Workers

A healthy economy is the most obvious and the best single remedy for labor market problems. In times of growth, unemployment, involuntary part-time employment, and the number of working poor all tend to fall. Economic growth alone, however, is only a partial solution of these problems. Two economic trends—the rapid pace of technological change and the increased internationalization of the economy—directly influence the demand for low-wage workers.

Economic Trends

A healthy overall economy is the necessary foundation for alleviation of the problems of the working poor. When the economy prospers, labor markets tighten; hence, the opportunities of low-wage workers to find higher-paying jobs are enhanced. Strong economic growth helps the unemployed who have a better chance of finding jobs, and those involuntarily employed on a part-time basis who are more likely to find full-time jobs. Conversely, the labor market hardships experienced by the working poor are intensified during economic recession because the working poor tend to be employed in the least stable jobs.

The recent rise in the number and percentage of working poor reflects the upward drift in the overall unemployment rate. The number and percentage of workers living in poverty fell sharply during the late 1960s when the unemployment rate dipped below 4 percent and the real value of the minimum wage was at its highest level. This percentage continued to fall in the early 1970s when the unemployment rate ranged between 4.8 and 5.5 percent. With the 1974-75 recession, the poverty rate of workers rose. During the subsequent recovery and as the unemployment rate fell, the concurrence of work and poverty dropped to all-time lows of 2.1 percent for full-time year-round workers and 5.7 percent of all workers in 1979.

The number of working poor jumped sharply after 1979 as a consequence of two recessions and as the unemployment rate hit a post–World War II high in 1982. When the unemployment rate dropped to the 7 percent range in 1984 and 1985, the number of workers who were poor fell only slightly. More sustained economic growth and tighter labor markets are apparently necessary before the benefits reach more of the working poor.

The most positive aspect of the labor market in recent years has been the tremendous growth in the overall number of jobs. This

growth is in sharp contrast with the relatively stagnant employment levels of other industrial countries. Although the rate of
United States job creation has been slower in the 1980s than in the
previous two decades, almost 11 million net new jobs were created
from the beginning of 1980 until the end of 1986. Because of the
fast rate of growth in the labor force, however, the unemployment
rate remains high. In addition, as the rising number of working
poor indicates, an increase in the number of jobs does not necessarily correspond to improved conditions for all workers.

Uneven Growth

Economic growth bypasses large segments of the working poor
because of employment barriers. Such barriers include the mismatch between their limited skills and the skills required in the
available jobs. The working poor may also not be affected by
overall economic growth because of their geographic isolation.
Labor surplus areas may remain relatively unaffected by nationwide economic trends. There may be opportunities only for those
unemployed who are willing or able to migrate to more prosperous areas.

Rural poverty has often proved intractable even in the presence
of nationwide economic expansion. In metropolitan areas, uneven
development is also common. The suburban economy can flourish
while the central city's languishes, and pockets of poverty often
exist side by side with booming development. In recent years,
many cities have had a renaissance, new skyscrapers dot the
horizon, and revitalized commercial markets continue to spring
up, but this prosperity does not necessarily benefit the working
poor. Based on a 1986 analysis of the New York City economy, the
chairman of the Regional Plan Association concluded: "More
than anywhere else in the country, we are creating a two-tier
society of the haves and have nots." The report cited mismatch
between the skills required for the new jobs and the skills pos-
sessed by the unemployed or low wage workers as a primary
reason for the uneven development.[4]

The working poor are also concentrated in industries whose
prosperity is only loosely linked to general economic trends. The
woes of workers in industries such as agriculture or textiles con-

tinued during the economic recovery that began in 1983 and continued in 1987.

This evidence has led to a debate over whether a two-tier economy is polarizing American labor markets. This discussion is directly related to the fate of the working poor because, if middle-income jobs decline, more workers will be pushed into the low-wage job market and fewer will escape it. Some analysts argue that high-paying manufacturing jobs are declining while low-paying service jobs are on the rise. They suggest, further, that technological change as well as international competition will exacerbate this situation.

Proponents of the two-tier economy theory tend to overstate their case. The problems of low-wage workers are indeed growing, uneven development is a fact of the American economy, and American industry clearly no longer dominates the world economy as it once did, but this situation does not mean that middle-income jobs are declining or will soon entirely disappear from the American labor market.

Technological Change

The claim that new technology eliminates middle-income jobs rests on two assumptions. The first is that high technology industries—such as computers or communications—provide many high- and low-wage jobs, but few opportunities for middle-wage workers. The second assumption is that new technology displaces workers as computers replace administrative personnel and clerks while robots replace low- or semiskilled factory workers.

Evidence in support of these assumptions is lacking, however. The growth of high technology industries does not necessarily bode ill for low-wage workers. High technology industries still comprise only a relatively small proportion of employment (6.2 percent in 1982 by one definition), and the pay scale is good. There is a high proportion of highly paid workers, production workers are well paid, and there are few low-paid jobs.[5] The increase of high-wage jobs in high technology industries will not, however, expand opportunities for low-skilled workers who are unqualified. The working poor would benefit more from these industries if lower-skilled, lower-paying jobs—that would nevertheless pay above poverty wages—were to be created.

Dislocation of workers by new technology has been an issue since the dawn of production. Technology does displace workers and tends to raise skill requirements, and policies are needed to help the transition of displaced workers to new employment. But technology is also the engine of progress: it raises productivity and increases the standard of living. The creation of new products and new markets then generates employment growth.

More specifically, advances in technology do not necessarily work to the detriment of low-wage workers. First, even technology that directly displaces workers may, in the long run, save or create more jobs. A firm's competitiveness may depend on technological changes, so the choice may be between losing some jobs by making those changes (or actually gaining jobs, if the reduction in costs leads to an increase in demand) or losing many more jobs by not making the changes.

Second, new technology which eliminates some tasks does not always cause a direct loss of jobs. The restructuring of the production process may create new tasks for the displaced workers. Third, a major reason for the decline in the competitiveness of United States industries has been the slow rate of productivity growth since the early 1970s. The argument that new technology has been introduced too quickly is not persuasive. On the contrary, it seems that new technology has not been introduced fast enough to spur economic growth.

International Competition

In contrast to the uncertain effects of technological change on the low-wage labor market, the rise of international competition has created employment problems for both workers in general and low-wage workers in particular. International trade plays an unprecedented role in the United States and world economy. In 1985, United States merchandise imports and exports accounted for 14 percent of the gross national product, nearly double the amount two decades earlier. In part because of the decline in transportation and communication costs, goods can now be produced (depending on factor costs such as labor) anywhere in the world, and then shipped elsewhere.

The United States economy benefits from trade both because

exports provide jobs and because imports provide a wider range of goods, frequently at cheaper prices. The increased international-ization of the world economy has, however, been a mixed blessing for the United States economy. The huge jump in the trade deficit resulted in a net employment loss from cutbacks in domestic pro-duction estimated to run as high as 3 million. In addition, inter-national competition dampens the growth of wages in this coun-try because firms cut costs in an attempt to remain competitive while workers accept lower wages in fear of the alternative—no wage at all.

It is the relatively unskilled United States workers who often face the brunt of these negative effects of international competi-tion. Low-skill jobs can be easily transferred abroad. In many cases, firms resort to outward processing—part of a product is assembled here, sent elsewhere for the production requiring low-skilled labor-intensive work, and then the nearly completed or finished product is imported back into this country. Outward pro-cessing imports grew at an annual rate of 20 percent from 1966 to 1983. The employment loss in low-wage industries can be signifi-cant.[6] Employment in the low-wage apparel and textile industries dropped from 1.44 million workers in 1973 to 1.11 million work-ers by mid-1986. Some of the displaced workers are forced to join the ranks of the working poor, and the exporting of jobs dimin-ishes their employment opportunities.

Policies to enhance this country's economic competitiveness should not focus on reducing wages. Even low-wage American workers cannot compete internationally on the basis of wages alone, particularly when the competition tends to be workers in third world nations whose wages are a fraction of the United States' minimum wage.

Job Trends

Analysts who argue that relatively fewer high-paying jobs are being created cite as evidence the shift from goods-producing to service-producing employment. (Goods-producing industries pri-marily comprise manufacturing firms, but also include mining and construction. Service-producing industries are transportation and public utilities; wholesale trade; retail trade; finance, insur-ance, and real estate; services; and government.) Between 1970 and 1986, 95 percent of the 29.3 million net new nonagriculture jobs were in the service sectors. Between 1980 and 1986, the service sectors added 10.5 million jobs, whereas the number employed in the goods-producing industries dropped by 0.7 million. This trend is expected to continue. The Bureau of Labor Statistics has estimated that 90 percent of the growth in the number of jobs from 1984 to 1995 will be in the service sector.[7]

This ongoing shift from a goods-based economy to a service-based economy is a matter of concern because millions of dislocated workers experience difficulties in finding new jobs and in regaining the level of earnings they had in their former jobs. The Department of Labor estimated that from January 1981 to January 1986 almost 11 million workers aged twenty years and over lost their jobs as a result of plant closings or mass layoffs. Almost 40 percent of these workers had been at their jobs for more than three years.[8]

On the other hand, this transition from goods-producing to service-producing employment does not mean the demise of middle-wage jobs. Although manufacturing jobs pay more on average than service sector jobs, the wage levels of many lost manufacturing jobs were below the average for total private industry. The service sectors, moreover, include jobs as diverse as brain surgeon, lab technician, and nurse's aide. It does not follow, therefore, that growth in service industry jobs eliminates medium-wage jobs. The shift from goods-producing to service sector employment, even though it has been taking place at a faster pace in recent years, is also not a new trend. The percentage of service-producing jobs has increased steadily throughout this century.

The impact of these industrial and occupational trends on the increasing number of working poor is uncertain. The decline in low-skilled but relatively high-paying manufacturing production jobs is likely to create more working poor. However, employment in some low-wage occupations is also declining. The number of individuals working in agriculture has continued to decline throughout the twentieth century. The number of household workers is also falling.

Other low-paying service sector jobs, however, are increasing in number. The number of workers employed by eating and drinking establishments increased by 1.1 million from 1980 to 1985. The number of salesworkers, disproportionately represented among the working poor, has also been growing faster than other occupations. One controversial study claimed that three in five of the net new jobs that were created from 1979 to 1984 could be classified as low income compared to one in five from 1973 to 1979.[9] The dramatic shift can in part be explained by the fall in the real value of the minimum wage (a full-time year-round minimum-wage worker could fall in the study's low-income stratum in 1984 but not in 1979) and by an increase in part-time workers who have low annual earnings.

The correct interpretation of job growth trends for low-wage workers is elusive. Is it to the benefit of agricultural employees that their number is declining? Though this may mean that there are fewer low-wage workers in this industry, unless the displaced workers find better positions elsewhere, the trend may not be a positive one overall. Similarly, some analysts focus on the large growth of relatively low-paying service sector occupations, and argue that this is evidence of worsening labor market conditions. If these jobs were not available, however, low-skilled workers might not have other employment options.

To some extent, then, the discussion of trends in the low-wage job market inevitably raises broader questions concerning economic growth and government policies. If the choice is no job growth versus job growth at low wages, the latter is preferable. The economy may have a greater number of low-wage workers but more workers will be employed. Another kind of growth is obviously preferable—growth in jobs with reasonably high wages.

The Supply of Low-Wage Workers

Changes in the supply of workers traditionally employed in low-wage labor markets influence working conditions in those markets. In the language of economists, all things being equal, the rise in the supply of labor is likely to reduce wages, increase unemployment, or, at least, moderate increases in pay levels. Immigrants, women, and youth are three groups that tend to congregate in low-wage markets.

Immigration

Since the mid-1960s, large numbers of immigrants have entered the United States. In 1980, the 14.1 million resident foreign-born individuals accounted for 6.2 percent of the total population, as compared to 4.8 percent a decade earlier. Some 570,000 immigrants legally entered the country in 1985. Net migration into the United States accounted for 13 percent of the population growth in the 1960s, 20 percent in the 1970s, and a projected 25 percent from 1984 to 1995.[10] Estimates of the numbers of illegal immigrants living in the United States vary widely, ranging from a low of 3 million to a high of 12 million.

Immigration can spur economic growth. Immigrants contribute productive resources and increase consumption, both of which can eventually lead to job creation. They often pay more in taxes than they receive in government services. Over the long run, permanent immigrants are unlikely to be disproportionately represented among the poor.[11]

From a broad perspective, the economy's adjustment to the influx of large numbers of immigrants, particularly those who enter the country legally and who remain for long periods, proceeds fairly smoothly. This comforting conclusion does not, however, apply to all situations. The concentration of immigrants, whether legal or undocumented, in specific labor markets can exacerbate not only their own adjustment problems but also those of other workers in the same communities. Illegal immigrants in particular frequently work under the most difficult conditions and they may negatively influence the situation of other low-wage workers. There is little agreement on the extent of this influence, in part because counts of the number of illegals as well as studies of their characteristics and occupations are imprecise. Moreover, some analysts believe that illegals are in job markets separate from legal workers, that employers recruit illegal immigrants to perform jobs shunned by native workers.[12] Others believe that both illegal and legal immigrants directly compete with native-born workers for jobs, and that this competition is especially fierce in low-skilled occupations.[13]

Undocumented aliens tend to be younger and less skilled then legal immigrants. They are found in a wide range of industries

and occupations but are concentrated in low-skilled low-wage occupations such as farm worker or nonfarm laborer. Employers
sometimes seek out undocumented aliens because they are willing to work under substandard conditions. Illegal immigrants are
not likely to complain to authorities about abusive conditions
because they are subject to deportation; they are an easy target
for employer exploitation.

Not all illegal immigrants work for low wages under hazardous
labor conditions, but the rise of sweatshops employing undocumented aliens in Los Angeles, New York, and other cities suggests that working conditions usually associated with the early
twentieth century still exist for illegal immigrants today. Such
working conditions are not only difficult for illegal immigrants
(though they may well be preferable to conditions in their native
countries), they may also lower the wages and other working
conditions of legal low-wage workers. When employers can hire a
"shadow class" of workers at a low wage and deny them other
legally mandated minimal work conditions, the demand for legal
labor falls and employment conditions may deteriorate.

As the number of immigrants, legal and illegal, has risen in a
time of loose labor markets, the debate over United States immigration policy has intensified. At the end of the 1986 legislative
session, Congress broke a long impasse and adopted a comprehensive immigration reform bill. The new law established sanctions
against employers who knowingly hire undocumented workers,
granted amnesty and citizenship to illegal immigrants who could
prove continuous residence in the United States since January
1982, and included special provisions for some agricultural workers that enable them to obtain temporary employment status.
Whether the law will radically alter the flow of immigrants remains to be seen. The Immigration and Naturalization Service in
the Department of Justice is responsible for the enforcement of
immigration laws. It is generally recognized that the service
lacks sufficient resources to execute its responsibilities adequately.

Women and Youth

The increasing numbers of women and youth in the work force
have often been cited as part of the cause of both the rising unem-

ployment rate and the low rate of wage growth. Historically these groups have had higher rates of unemployment than adult men (although in recent years the incidence of unemployment among women and men has converged) and have tended to be employed in low-wage job markets. Women are overrepresented among part-time workers who remain in poverty.

In the 1980s, the growth of women in the labor force has continued whereas the number of youth has declined. The number of women in the labor force jumped 8 million from 1975 to 1980 and rose by another 6.6 million in the next six years. Even though the crystal ball of the Bureau of Labor Statistics may be cloudy at times, its projection for the next decade may turn out to be on the mark. Women will continue to account for a disproportionately large share of future labor force growth, albeit at a slower rate than in the past. In the future, however, women may be less heavily concentrated in the low-wage labor market if their attachment to the work force stabilizes and if sex discrimination declines.

The situation of single women who head families is likely to remain a matter of special concern to policy makers. This group has been subject to inordinately high poverty rates. Their earnings problems are often enduring and the factors leading to the formation of single-parent families are complex.

Now that most of the post–World War II baby boom generation has entered the work force, the supply of youths available for low-wage jobs will continue to decrease. There were 1.7 million fewer individuals aged sixteen to twenty-four in the labor force in 1985 than in 1980; by 1995, the figure is expected to drop by another 3.4 million. The decline in the number of youth may cause employers to raise wages at the low end of the labor market but, as the labor force becomes more dominated by prime-age workers, the competition for good full-time jobs will intensify and upward mobility paths will be more difficult to navigate. Women accounted for 63 percent of the labor force growth between 1975 and 1985 (Table 4).

Though the job prospects for most youth may improve through the rest of this decade, the unemployment rate of minority teenagers, which averaged 36 percent in 1986, is likely to remain high because of their lack of skills, the location of jobs, and discrimina-

Table 4. Women and youth in the labor force between 1975 and 1995 (in millions)

	Actual			Estimate	
	1975	*1980*	*1985*	*1990*	*1995*
Total labor force	93.8	106.9	115.5	122.7	129.2
Women	37.5	45.5	51.1	55.5	59.9
% of labor force	40.0%	42.6%	44.2%	45.2%	46.4%
16–24 year olds	22.6	25.3	23.6	21.3	20.2
% of labor force	24.1%	23.7%	20.4%	17.4%	15.6%

Source: Bureau of Labor Statistics.

tion. Changing trends in the numbers of women and youth in the labor force will not completely ameliorate their labor market problems.

Overall, the labor force is projected to increase 12 percent from 1985 to 1995, which is half the growth rate of 1975 to 1985. The number of women is expected to increase through 1995, but also at half the pace of growth from 1975 to 1985. The continued decrease in young workers helps explain the slower overall rate of growth.

Whither the Low-Wage Job Market?

Some of the trends in the low-wage job market are positive. In contrast to other industrialized countries, the United States has been remarkably successful in generating additional job opportunities. If the economy continues to generate jobs at the rate it did during past decades, and if women enter the work force at slower rates and the supply of youth declines, free market forces are likely to improve the employment conditions of the remaining low-skilled workers. This assumes that a rise in the supply of immigrants does not outweigh the diminished supply of native youth.

Other trends are less positive. In early 1987, after more than four years of recovery from the 1981–82 recession, the unemployment rate remained at a higher level at the positive stage of the business cycle than during any other post–World War II recovery. Persistent high unemployment, with whole regions and industries bypassed by overall economic growth, indicates ongoing problems for the working poor. International competition has directly increased the number of low-wage workers through the decreased use of unskilled but relatively high-paid workers as well as by its general dampening effect on wages. The damage to native workers caused by immigrants is often overstated, but large concentrations of low-skilled immigrants in selected labor markets can not only exacerbate their own difficult working conditions but can also undermine the working conditions of other low-wage workers.

The impact of unions is conspicuously absent from this discussion of the low-wage labor market. In part due to the greater difficulty in organizing low-wage workers, unions play a minor role in low-wage labor markets, except in the garment and service industries. Unions have taken some steps to organize low-wage retail and service workers, but progress has been slow.

Much of our analysis points to the need for more effective government policies aimed at reducing the number of low-wage workers and at improving the conditions they face in the labor market. Federal macroeconomic policy has been focused on driving down inflation, at the cost of high unemployment rates, thus contributing to the hardships of low-wage workers. With substantial slack in the economy, federal monetary policy could focus on driving down the unemployment rate without renewing an inflationary spiral.

A careful balance needs to be struck in both trade and immigration policies. Trade policies should be designed to consider not only the victims of international competition but also its benefits to consumers, to trading partners, and to international relations. Immigration policies should attempt to ease the hardships faced by low-wage workers but should also consider that this nation has grown not in spite of but because of immigration. Welcoming those who hope to share in our freedom and high standard of living should also be a goal.

Targeted programs to assist poor workers aid those left behind by economic growth. In secondary labor markets in which competition is fierce and unions are absent, the federal government is the major and sometimes the only force that can help these workers obtain reasonable working conditions and a decent minimum wage. The federal government can supply the resources needed to raise the skill levels of workers and can help knock down barriers created by discrimination. It can aid the job search process and counteract persistent job deficits. Federal programs can also provide income and service support to those workers unable to escape poverty on their own. In short, active and effective federal intervention not only can, but is essential to, improving the oppressive employment conditions of the working poor.

3

Federal Policies

4. Making Work Pay

The federal government directly influences working conditions through its minimum-wage and tax policies. The minimum wage helps workers earn adequate levels of income, and tax policies determine how much of that income they retain. The judicious application of these policies increases the net income of low-wage workers, alleviates deprivation, and sustains the incentive to work.

The working poor and other low-wage workers who lack bargaining power must rely on government action to set a floor under their wages. In the 1980s this floor dropped considerably. Minimum-wage earnings in 1986 for a full-time year-round worker provided income equivalent to only four-fifths of the poverty line for a family of three.

Federal policies in the first half of the 1980s had a negative effect on the position of the working poor. Not only did inflation erode the value of the minimum wage, but the working poor had to pay substantially more in taxes. The 1986 tax reform bill provided substantial relief to the working poor: the standard deduction, the personal exemption, and the earned income tax credit were each raised, thus reducing or eliminating the taxes of millions of the working poor.

Minimum Wage

The need for a federal minimum-wage floor became clear during the first few decades of this century. The unregulated market system did not lead to minimally acceptable living standards for significant numbers of the work force. Existing state regulation of wages was limited and ineffective. These factors resulted in the passage of the Fair Labor Standards Act of 1938 which set a national wage standard for the first time in American history. Since then, Congress has increased the minimum-wage level on six occasions and coverage has been extended to the bulk of all nonsupervisory employees. Congress passed the latest round of minimum-wage amendments in 1977, when it raised the hourly rate in four steps, reaching $3.35 in 1981. It remained at the same level six years later.

The minimum-wage law directly and indirectly affects millions of workers. In 1986, about 1.6 million salaried and 5.1 million hourly workers earned the minimum wage or less. Almost six million more workers received wages just above this level. Some low-wage employers who pay above the minimum link raises to the level of the federal standard.

| | Hourly earnings, 1986 | | |
	Total	*Below minimum*	*At minimum*	*$3.36–3.99*
Workers (in millions)	96.9	3.3	3.5	5.8

Minimum-wage workers tend to be part-time workers and women; almost two-thirds of minimum-wage workers are in either category. As a result, the level of the minimum wage often directly influences female-headed households. Although a disproportionately high number of minimum-wage workers are black, more than four in five minimum-wage workers are white.[1] Contrary to a common misconception, most minimum-wage workers are not teenagers in their first job. Only 31 percent are teenagers, another 21 percent are twenty to twenty-four years old, and 48 percent are twenty-five years or older. Twenty-eight percent of all minimum-wage workers are heads of household and another 28 percent are spouses. Millions of minimum-wage workers play a central role in providing a decent standard of living for their families.

Minimum-wage workers are found in a broad array of occupations, although they tend to be concentrated in the service industries, agriculture, and retail trade—all industries that employ a high proportion of the working poor. Three of every four private household workers earn the minimum or less, and one of every three service workers (other than private household) is employed at or below the minimum, as are nearly half of all farm laborers and one in five of all sales workers.[2] Some employers or occupations remain exempt from minimum-wage requirements.

The earnings of poor workers tend to cluster around minimum-wage levels. One in four impoverished workers receiving hourly rates in March 1985 earned the minimum wage or less. Another one in three of these workers earned between $3.36 and $4.35 an hour. However, four out of five workers earning the minimum wage escape poverty, primarily because other earners supplement family income.[3] Most working poor earn near the minimum wage but most minimum-wage workers are not poor. The appropriate level of the minimum wage must be judged in light of its effects on workers from both poverty and nonpoverty families.

A Sinking Floor

By any measure, the 1986 minimum wage provided a historically low level of support. Adjusted for inflation, the statutory hourly wage rate was at its lowest level since 1955. The minimum wage rose in real terms until 1968, stabilized in the 1970s, and fell sharply after 1979. In 1986, the real wage was 20 percent less than its average in the 1970s and a third less than its peak in 1968 (Figure 6).

The Reagan administration opposed increasing the minimum wage and Congress followed its lead, despite the fact that prices rose by 27 percent during the six years following the 1981 increase. As a result, the minimum wage slipped below 40 percent of the average hourly wage for nonsupervisory private, nonagricultural workers for the first time since 1949. In the 1950s and the 1960s, Congress generally set the minimum wage at about 50 percent of the average wage in private industry.

Minimum-wage income is only enough to raise some individuals above the poverty threshold. In 1986 a full-time year-round minimum-wage worker earned $6,968 in a year—$1,800 less than the poverty threshold of $8,738 for a family of three and $4,200 less than the poverty threshold of $11,200 for a family of four. In contrast, throughout most of the 1960s and the 1970s, the minimum

Figure 6. The real value of the minimum wage has declined sharply in the 1980s.

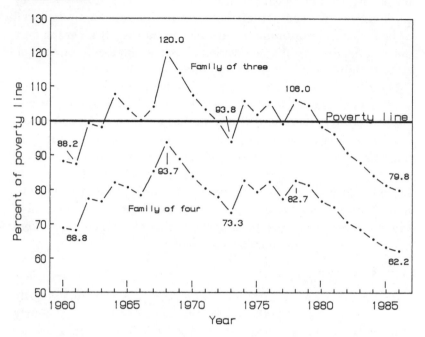

Source: U.S. Department of Labor

wage was sufficient to bring a family of three out of poverty (Figure 7). As the real value of the minimum wage declined since 1978, it is no surprise that the number of working poor rose.

As the federal minimum sank to historic lows, seven states and the District of Columbia raised their minimums above $3.35 an hour. These actions have affected only a small minority of minimum-wage workers. Moreover, in real terms, the statutory minimum wage in these states is still below historic levels. Federal action strengthening the minimum wage would provide more substantial support for the working poor and other low-wage workers.

A Cracked Floor

As testified to by the 3.3 million workers who earned less than the minimum wage in 1986, the wage floor does not protect all workers. The self-employed are not covered; in addition, exemp-

Figure 7. Minimum wage earnings for a full-time year-round worker have fallen well below the poverty line for a three-member family.

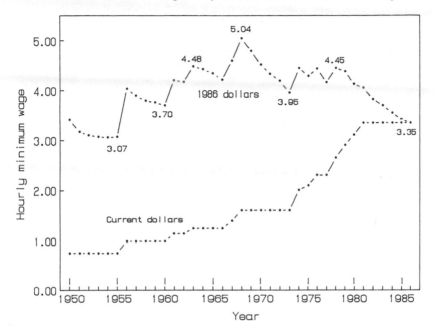

Source: U.S. Department of Labor

tions in the law apply to ten million private nonsupervisory employees. Many employees are denied minimum-wage earnings not because of exemptions, but because of employer noncompliance. Poor workers are presumably highly represented among these groups, although precise breakouts of the number employed in uncovered sectors or who are illegally paid less than the minimum wage are unavailable. Moreover, with the exception of the self-employed who may be experiencing a low-earnings year, below-minimum wage positions are unlikely to provide opportunities for future earnings growth.

The proportion of workers covered by the minimum wage has increased considerably since the law's inception. The 1938 Fair Labor Standards Act covered only one in four workers, compared with 87 percent of all private nonsupervisory employees in 1985. As a result of a 1985 Supreme Court decision in *Garcia v. San*

Antonio Metropolitan Transit Authority, state and local employees are now covered by the federal minimum-wage standard.

Of the 10.5 million nonsupervisory employees lacking minimum-wage coverage in 1985, 6.3 million were employed in the retail trade or service industries; 1.2 million in finance, insurance, and real estate; 1 million in agriculture; and 500,000 in private households (Table 5). The 2.6 million outside sales workers employed in a variety of industries are also exempt from FLSA coverage.

The retail trade and service business exemption affects the largest number of workers. Establishments with total annual sales of $362,500 or less are not required to pay the minimum wage. In 1978, this exemption excluded 4.2 million workers from minimum-wage protection. One-quarter of these workers earned less than the minimum wage.[4]

Some workers do not receive the minimum wage because they are exempt from coverage, but others are illegally underpaid. In 1985 the Department of Labor identified $30 million in unpaid wages because of violations of the minimum wage. Employers agreed to pay $19 million of the wages owed to 139,000 employees. Only 3 percent of establishments subject to the FLSA are inspected each year and almost all inspections are made in response to employee complaints. Fines are mere slaps on the wrist; in most cases,

Table 5. Nonsupervisory private-sector employees, September 1985 (in millions)

	Covered by FLSA	Exempt
Total	63.0	10.5
Agriculture	.6	1.0
Manufacturing	16.8	.5
Wholesale trade	4.0	1.0
Retail trade	13.4	2.5
Finance, insurance, and real estate	3.9	1.2
Service industries	13.2	3.8
Private household	1.1	.5
Other	10.1	.1

Source: U.S. Department of Labor, Employment Standards Administration
Note: Details do not add to totals because of rounding off.

an employer is obliged to pay only the difference between the actual amount paid and the amount that is due under the minimum wage. In rare instances, employers are required to pay double that amount.

The Minimum Wage Study Commission estimated that in 1979 only about one-fifth of the underpayments resulting from FLSA violations were detected. Over 70 percent of total minimum-wage violations occurred under the provision that allows employers to deduct costs of meals, lodging, and other expenses customarily provided to minimum-wage workers. These violations are sometimes due to technical mistakes in calculating wages and not to willful violations of the law.[5] The percentage of violations currently detected is probably even lower, as both the number of man-hours spent on enforcement and the level of fines dropped in the 1980s.

Although some of the violations of the minimum wage are trivial in nature, other violations should be cause for concern. In 1982, the Labor Standards Subcommittee of the House Education and Labor Committee found widespread evidence of sweatshops in the needle trades. The subcommittee chairman described an employee-employer relationship in these sweatshops as follows: "An under-educated, underskilled, usually illegal worker is compelled by economic desperation to work under intolerable, less than subsistence conditions, abused and unprotected from the most fundamental forms of industrial exploitation."[6] In addition to the effect on workers, legitimate employers are placed at a competitive disadvantage when other employers illegally pay less than the minimum wage.

The extent of sweatshops and the size of their employment force is unknown. Presumably many of these workers are poor, but they are not reflected in official statistics because they are not legal residents of the United States. Sweatshop workers usually do not report the illegal and inadequate conditions under which they work because they lack knowledge about labor laws, because they are afraid of losing their jobs, or because they fear deportation.

The increased use of workers at home, either in the needle trades or in newly developed arrangements in which a worker may be employed at home but be hooked up to the office via computer, compounds enforcement problems. Current staffing levels prevent federal officials from inspecting most businesses, let alone individual households. Enforcement could be strengthened if a greater effort was made to inspect potentially egregious offenders.

A Help or a Hindrance?

The appropriate level of the minimum wage has been the subject of intense dispute. Proponents argue that the minimum wage increases the standard of living and enhances the work ethic. Opponents argue that the minimum wage hurts low-wage employees because increases of hourly rates by government fiat reduce demand for workers and results in loss of jobs. The acid test is whether the benefits of high wages outweigh the negative effects of lost employment opportunities.

At the most fundamental level, the minimum wage is a statement by society that work conditions below a given standard are unacceptable. The need for government intervention to mandate a minimal standard of living for workers reflects the reality that low-wage laborers are normally not in a position themselves to bargain for better working conditions. Most employees are protected from unreasonable work conditions either by unions, their own special skills, or benign employer practices. This is not often the case in low-wage labor markets which lack unions, in which workers lack skills and political clout, and in which employers are unlikely to adopt beneficent standard labor practices. Federal intervention helps to bring the work conditions in these labor markets up to socially required standards.

Many individuals and families benefit from the higher wages that result from the mandated minimum. The wage floor helps some escape poverty and lessens its impact on others. For minimum-wage earners who are not poor, the extra income is often essential. A teenager can save more money to pay for rising school costs or a multi-earner family may scrape together enough money to purchase more than the bare necessities.

Studies of the minimum wage tend to focus on its employment effects and ignore its equally important income effects. The limited evidence that is available does indicate, however, that the income effects have been substantial, and that especially among adult females, they overshadow the expected job loss.[7] In 1981, when the hourly minimum wage was raised from $3.10 to $3.35, the Department of Labor estimated that the potential aggregate annual increase amounted to \$2.2 billion, and that 5.5 million workers were eligible to receive raises. The income effects in other years were of equivalent size.

Another salutary impact of the minimum wage is that it encourages individuals to work rather than depend on welfare. When individuals earn income instead of relying on government support, they not only benefit from the satisfaction of helping themselves, but their possibilities for future advancement are enhanced. Society benefits both from the increased output and the reduction in welfare costs. An inadequate statutory minimum wage may discourage the poor from seeking employment. When the working poor toil for little gain, work can be seen as a less desirable and futile alternative to welfare.

Statutory increases in the minimum wage do result in some job losses; workers can be priced out of the market when the wage is set by government fiat. However, minimum-wage opponents tend to overstate both the extent of job loss and the applicability of free market theory to the functioning of low-wage labor markets. Economists have attempted to measure the employment loss from the statutory minimum wage, but because of the complexity of economic interactions, the quantitative results from these studies are subject to considerable imprecision. Nevertheless, a few general conclusions are warranted.

The minimum wage has the largest disemployment effect on young workers. The Minimum Wage Study Commission estimated that a 10 percent increase in the minimum wage decreases teenage employment opportunities by about 1 percent.[8] More recent analyses have supported this estimate.[9] The effect is greatest for those youths whose earnings are close to the minimum wage. Of course, the employment effect varies with economic conditions and demographic trends. The job loss among adults is less than that among youths. Adult labor markets are not so sensitive to minimum-wage changes as youth labor markets, both because youth workers are likely to be laid off before adult workers and because a smaller proportion of adults work at the minimum.

Quantitative estimates of job losses caused by the minimum wage are ballpark guesses. Objections to a statutory floor under wages are grounded more in free market theory than in empirical evidence. According to that theory, by arbitrarily setting the minimum wage above the wage workers would otherwise receive, the demand for workers drops and the supply of workers rises because potentially higher earnings induce more workers to seek jobs. The inevitable result, according to the opponents of a standard minimum wage, is that fewer workers are employed and the unemployment rate rises.

In practice, this theory may not be reflected in the actions of either employers or employees. Higher wages may enhance job stability and commitment among workers. Employers, in turn, may respond by reorganizing production processes to make better use of their existing employees. As a result of increased productivity, the actual cost of labor may not rise so much as the cost of the minimum wage. Also, since minimum-wage firms compete with one another, raising the minimum wage for all firms, as long as coverage is complete and enforcement is effective, will not give one firm a competitive advantage over another.

Some firms set their pay scales at the minimum wage which in some areas may be below the market clearing price. In these cases, raising the wage would actually increase employment because workers who would turn down jobs at lower wages might accept them at a higher pay. At least to some extent, firms have adjusted their wages upward in the absence of a minimum-wage increase,[10] but market reactions are not so quick and smooth as predicted by free market theorists. Minimum-wage employers are reluctant to raise their pay scales absent a federally mandated requirement.

The minimum wage has scant impact on overall economic conditions. Little noticeable effect on unemployment has followed increases in the hourly rate. In the 1950s and the 1960s, when the minimum wage rose in real terms, the unemployment rate remained low. In the 1970s and the first half of the 1980s, the wage floor sank but the sinking did not prevent high levels of unemployment. Similarly, since the vast majority of workers earn considerably more than the minimum wage, it has only a minuscule effect on the inflation rate. In any event, workers who earn the minimum wage should not shoulder a disproportionate financial burden in the fight against inflation.

A prudent minimum wage policy must balance the prevention of job losses with the benefits of eliminating unacceptably low rewards for labor. If the minimum wage is too high, the working poor and other minimum-wage workers may indeed suffer more than they gain. Nearly a half century of federal experience with the minimum wage offers persuasive evidence that if the floor under wages is set at one-half of the average hourly pay of nonsupervisory workers, the resulting disemployment effects remain insignificant and the accompanying income boosts are instrumental in alleviating deprivation and in encouraging economic self-sufficiency. The task for Congress is to strike the right balance between employment and income effects.

Youth Subminimum

A subminimum wage for teenagers has been proposed in an effort to drive down the high youth unemployment rate. Advocates of this approach argue that the minimum wage has its highest disemployment effect on the young, preventing them from acquiring essential employment experience. Teenagers, it is argued, do not require wages as high as adults. The Reagan administration proposed a "youth opportunity wage" equal to 75 percent of the minimum wage. The administration estimated that lowering the cost of hiring youths would create 400,000 jobs for youths. By April 1987, the real value of the minimum wage was 30 percent lower than when President Reagan took office and the number of youths entering the labor market had also declined. Yet teenage unemployment remained at high levels, creating doubts that further cuts in the minimum wage would in fact generate added employment opportunities.

A subminimum is already in effect for some young workers. Since 1961, employers have been able to obtain Department of Labor certification to hire full-time students at 85 percent of the minimum wage as long as these students work less than twenty hours a week. In fiscal 1985, an estimated 195,800 students were certified for employment under this program.

Employers of economically disadvantaged youths are also eligible for a 40 percent wage subsidy under the Targeted Jobs Tax Credit. For disadvantaged sixteen to seventeen year olds in summer employment, the subsidy is substantially more generous and amounts to an 85 percent tax credit. If lower wages are essential to induce employers to hire economically disadvantaged youths, the TJTC not only reduces wages more than a youth subminimum wage would, but has the advantage of providing more income to the targeted youths. Furthermore, youths from poor families who have trouble breaking into the labor force tend to lack skills and connections to the job market. Lower wages will not necessarily induce employers to hire these youths; they need to master the three Rs and they require specialized programs, such as the Job Corps, to prepare them for the job market.

Not only would the subminimum result in an income loss for many youths, it could well harm the working poor and other adults who work at the minimum wage, because some young workers would be substituted for older workers. The Minimum Wage Study Commission, which opposed a youth subminimum wage, speculated that a youth subminimum set at 75 percent of the adult minimum would create 400,000 to 450,000 jobs for youths but would also displace 50,000 to 150,000 adult workers. The commission noted that this displacement estimate is low because its analysis implicitly examined the possibility of youth replacing average adult workers instead of examining the more likely effect that adult workers earning the minimum wage or slightly higher would be displaced.[11] Additionally, the job creation figures must be viewed with some skepticism because youths have alternative uses for their time. In some labor markets, there is mounting evidence that their reservation wage is higher than the current minimum wage, let alone the proposed subminimum.

Reforms

Restoring the minimum wage to its traditional level of support—50 percent of the average nonsupervisory private hourly wage—would require as of early 1987 a 32 percent increase or about $1.07 per hour. At whatever level the minimum wage is set, its protection is sharply diminished if exemptions are common and if the law is not enforced. Strengthening the minimum-wage standard will not lift all of the working poor out of poverty. A sizable proportion of the full-time year-round working poor are self-employed or otherwise uncovered by the minimum-wage law and part-time minimum-wage workers may still have annual earnings below the poverty line. Nevertheless, some individuals would be raised above the poverty threshold by a higher mini-

mum wage and others, though remaining in poverty, would receive necessary additional income. Though most minimum-wage
workers are not poor, they, too, would benefit from a raise.

Federal Taxes

The disposable income of the working poor depends, of course,
not only on the wages they receive but on their tax burden. In the
first half of the 1980s, federal tax policy contributed to the deteriorating situation of the working poor. The minimum wage declined considerably whereas the taxes of low-wage workers rose
substantially. The 1986 tax bill, however, provided relief to low-
income workers; it restored the effective federal tax rate of low
earners to the level of the late 1970s.

Structure

The three largest components of the federal tax system are the
personal income tax, the social security tax, and the corporate
income tax. A goal of the progressive structure of the personal
income tax has been to minimize the obligations of low-wage
earners. The social security tax has been a greater burden on the
poor. This rate has risen considerably over time and, in addition,
workers pay the same rate from the first dollar they earn annually up to the $43,800 they earn. (The maximum social security
tax base of $43,800 in 1987 is adjusted annually for inflation.)
The corporate income tax affects the poor only indirectly through
goods consumption, but it is generally considered to be a progressive tax; its costs are borne more by the owners of the business
than by the less well-to-do.[12]

In addition to the tax rate, three aspects of the federal personal
income tax system significantly affect the poor. The first, the
standard deduction, is the amount of earned income which is
exempt from any taxation. The standard deduction is available to
all taxpayers who do not itemize their deductions. A second aspect of the system that influences the amount of taxes paid by
low-wage workers is the personal exemption given for each individual covered by a tax return. A third key element of the tax
system for the poor is the earned income tax credit (EITC), enacted in 1975. In contrast to the standard deduction and personal

exemption which can be used by filers at all income levels, the EITC can be used only by low-income households with children. A tax credit is earned on a percentage of initial earnings and is phased out as earnings rise. If the credit exceeds personal income tax liability, the difference is refundable. The credit can, therefore, also offset the social security tax paid by low-wage workers.

Trends

Taxes are not considered in the calculation of the official poverty thresholds. Individuals and families who drop into poverty because of tax payments are not counted among the poor. The increase in the number of the officially counted working poor between 1979 and 1985 cannot be attributed to the higher taxes on low earners. Though taxes do not affect official poverty status, they obviously do affect the purchasing power of low earners.

Federal taxes paid by low-wage workers soared in the 1980s as social security taxes rose and as provisions benefiting low-wage workers failed to keep pace with inflation. When a deduction remains static, while both the cost of living and wages rise, the value of the deduction falls, thus increasing the effective tax rate at the poverty income level.

In 1979 a family of four was liable for the federal personal income tax when its income exceeded the poverty line by 16 percent; in 1986, the income tax threshold for this family was 17 percent *below* the poverty line. Combining the personal income tax with the social security payroll tax, the 1986 effective federal tax rate for a family of four with an annual income equal to the poverty threshold jumped nearly sixfold, from 1.8 percent to an estimated 10.6 percent. From 1979 to 1984 (the last year for which figures are available), the number of individuals whose incomes fell below the poverty line after payment of federal taxes increased from 675,000 to 2.4 million.[13]

Politicians of all stripes supported the 1986 tax bill with its beneficial provisions for the working poor. The tax bill raised the standard deduction, the personal exemption, and the earned income tax credit, and indexed the latter to inflation. The standard deduction and personal exemptions had been indexed to inflation as of 1985. For those earning less than $10,000 the 1986 bill cut

Table 6. Effective tax rate for family of four with poverty-level earnings

Year	Rate
1965	4.4%
1969	7.6
1973	6.6
1977	2.9
1979	1.8
1981	8.5
1983	9.8
1985	10.4
1988 (est).	2.1

Source: Center on Budget and Policy Priorities

the expected federal income tax liability by 57 percent in 1987 and 65 percent in 1988.[14] The percentage of income the poor must pay in personal income and payroll taxes returned to the levels of the late 1970s (Table 6).[15] The Center on Budget and Policy Priorities estimated that the tax cut would raise the income of a four-person family at the poverty level by greater than $1,000 or over 10 percent.[16]

The 1986 tax law also increased the standard deduction. The biggest effect was on single persons heading households.

	1986	*1988*
Joint return	$3,670	$5,000
Single heads of household	2,480	4,400
Single individual	2,480	3,000

The value of each personal exemption was almost doubled, increasing the $1,080 exemption in 1986 to $2,000 in 1989, and the earned income tax credit for low-wage workers was raised. In 1986, the EITC was equal to 11 percent of the first $5,000 in earnings (or a maximum credit of $550) and was phased out as earnings rose from $6,500 to $11,000. The credit benefited an estimated 6 million families to the tune of $2.1 billion, $1.4 billion of which was received as income tax refunds. Under the new tax law, the credit was increased to 14 percent of the first $5,714 in earnings (for a maximum credit of $800), and starts to phase out when earnings reach $9,000—its value declines to zero when earnings equal $17,000.

The 1986 tax law left unchanged many deductions that benefit middle-and upper-income filers, but that tend to be of little benefit to low-wage workers. For example, the generous mortgage interest deduction (totaling an estimated $27.6 billion in 1986) helps few low-income individuals because most working poor are unlikely to own their homes. The poor are also hardly in a position to take advantage of tax code provisions that encourage workers to save for the future; the poor need that money now. Whatever the merits of these deductions, they offer little assistance to the poor.

The 1986 tax act extended some assistance to low-wage workers in other areas. It included provisions that encourage employers to provide pension and health insurance benefits to low-wage workers. Under the new law, pension plans must cover a higher percentage of a firm's workers and the vesting period was reduced. A new tax credit was created for owners who lease units to low-income renters although other changes in the law may decrease investment in housing.

The 1986 tax bill provided tremendous benefits to the working poor, and because key provisions were indexed, the working poor will have low effective federal tax rates for the foreseeable future. A possible additional reform is extension of the EITC to single individuals or childless couples with low incomes who would benefit from a tax credit to offset their payroll taxes. The tax reform debate may now shift to the state and local level, where the poor are burdened by regressive state and local property and sales taxes.

Net Compensation

During the first half of the 1980s, two concurrent trends reduced the real income of the working poor. The minimum wage remained unchanged while taxes on those in poverty rose to historically high levels, increasing by almost 10 percent for a family of four with poverty level earnings. As of 1985, the net real income of low-wage workers was dramatically lower than in the late 1970s.

The 1986 tax bill reversed one of these trends by lowering taxes for the poor who will now keep almost all of the wages they earn. The challenge for the balance of the 1980s and beyond is to raise the real value of their earnings. If the minimum wage is raised to its traditional level, and thereupon is indexed and strictly enforced, the fruits of labor will be considerably more positive.

In lieu of raising the minimum wage, some analysts have proposed raising the earned income tax credit. This option would be targeted to the working poor; it would only increase the income of low-wage workers from poor families. Moreover, it would not discourage hiring because the direct cost of labor to employers would remain the same. The size of the credit could also vary by family size.[17]

Although a further expansion of the EITC would benefit the working poor, there would still be advantages to raising the minimum wage instead. First, low-wage workers who are not in poverty would also benefit from a raise in the minimum wage. Second, given the high federal deficit, increasing federal outlays and reducing revenues both present serious policy drawbacks. Raising the minimum wage, a private sector approach, also would provide the poor with more *earned* income, which is preferable to a large government income transfer. Third, and finally, a tax credit gives income at the end of the year but the poor require that income throughout the year.

Establishing labor conditions that will provide incentives to help lift workers out of poverty as a result of their own initiative is the best mechanism to improve the lot of the working poor. It is more preferable for workers to earn their way out of poverty than for the government to provide additional income support or in-kind benefits. The right mix of low federal taxes and an adequate federal minimum wage will establish labor conditions in which more workers can escape poverty on their own.

5. Removing Employment Obstacles

Many obstacles impede the poor's obtaining jobs that pay a decent wage. The general level of education has risen in the United States, but a large number of individuals who lack basic skills remain. These individuals have great difficulty competing in today's labor market and their difficulties are often transferred to the next generation. The children of the poor and unskilled are more likely than children from affluent families to be poorly prepared when they enter the work force.

The quality of the basic education system largely determines the skill levels of American workers. But even when proper educational facilities are available, some individuals fall through the cracks and require a second chance to acquire the basic skills necessary to compete for sustained employment in the labor market. Federal programs have played an important role in opening opportunities to the unskilled or handicapped adults and the need for such assistance has not diminished. The provision of basic skills can be seen as preventive medicine; the earning capacity of the working poor will be enhanced if they master the three Rs.

Some individuals who live in poverty have adequate job skills but are impeded by other barriers from finding or holding good jobs. For both women and minorities, discrimination remains a barrier to employment. Some of the poor require special support services; for example, the lack of adequate, affordable day care can be an insurmountable obstacle for a single parent with young children. Federal policies have addressed these problems through the enforcement of equal employment opportunity laws and the provision of social services.

Low Skills and Low Earnings

The level of workers' education or skills and their earnings are highly correlated. In 1984 college-educated householders aged twenty-five or older employed full time year round earned twice as much as individuals who completed only eight years of schooling and who worked full time.

Education	Median Income
Elementary	$17,387
High School	$26,238
College	$34,865

This general relationship between educational attainment and earnings does not hold for all groups. Women earn far less than men with similar educational attainments and blacks earn less than whites. Moreover, an analysis of educational attainment and earnings must also consider the level of education of the total labor supply. Increasing the education of person A, while keeping everyone else's education the same, will raise A's income more than if everyone's level of education was increased by an equivalent amount.

Nevertheless, there is a connection between the educational attainment of the work force and productivity; raising the education level of workers is likely to raise their incomes. Increasingly, a strong back alone is an insufficient employment skill as the job distribution in the economy continues to shift from the goods-producing to the service sector.

More specifically, the crucial need for many of the poor is acquisition of basic levels of competency in the three Rs. Private-sector training is generally geared to the specific needs of the business which leaves the task of providing basic skill training to the government. It is in the government's interest, but not necessarily a particular firm's interest, to provide general skill training that can be used in almost all jobs. A firm that provides general training will not benefit if the trained employees change companies.

The high level of educational attainment of today's work force is unprecedented. In 1950 only one-third of adults aged twenty-five or older had graduated from high school, by 1970 the figure jumped to over half, and by 1984 almost three out of four adults were high school graduates. Whether these increased years of education have led to equivalent increases in skill levels is a matter of widespread debate and justified concern.

The good news about rising years of average educational attainment should not obscure the problems confronting specific categories of individuals. The children of the poor and uneducated continue to be more likely to lack basic competency, often because of their unstimulating home environments and health problems. In addition, the poor often live in geographic areas where education funding and quality are inadequate. There are also millions of Americans who do not graduate from high school, are illiterate, or are disabled; all these groups are likely to experience difficulties in finding employment that will provide them with sufficient earnings to escape poverty.

School Leavers

Although one in seven poor persons has attended college, on average, the poor are less well educated than the nonpoor. Most telling, fewer than half of poor individuals age fifteen or older have graduated from high school. A General Accounting Office analysis found that, in October 1985, 4.3 million persons accounting for 13 percent of all individuals aged sixteen to twenty-four years were not enrolled in high school and lacked a high school diploma. Early school leaving among whites remained at a steady 13 to 14 percent from 1974 to 1985, whereas among blacks it declined from 21 percent to 16 percent. Since relatively fewer individuals completed high school before 1974, 27 percent of all adults aged twenty-five or over lacked high school degrees in 1984. The percentage of youths from households with low-income low-skilled earners who do not complete high school was three times the rate among youths from more affluent families.[1] Low educational attainment among the children of the poor and unskilled contributes to the persistence of the poverty cycle.

Individuals without high school degrees tend to lack skills and to experience economic and labor market hardship.[2] They experience higher unemployment rates than high school graduates, are less likely to seek work, and, if employed, earn lower wages in low-skilled jobs with poor work conditions. Further, the income gap between nongraduates and graduates has increased sharply since the 1960s; high school leavers have had a relatively more difficult time in the labor market than they had had previously.[3] This trend may be a result of rising educational requirements for jobs and the larger pool of high school graduates available to employers (even for those jobs that require limited skills). In such cases, the high school diploma serves as a screening device and indicates that the prospective employee has basic skills and can adjust to the discipline of the workplace.

Illiteracy

The number of years of education positively correlates with skill levels and with earnings, but only indirectly measures occupational skills. Some high school dropouts may have the same reading and math skills as high school graduates. The illiteracy rate is a reasonable measure of skill levels: individuals who fail to meet minimal competency levels generally lack skills. Employers do not necessarily need someone who is well versed in Shakespeare, but for most jobs they require workers with basic reading, writing, and mathematical proficiency. Basic competency is essential to function effectively in today's labor market, even in most entry level jobs. Low competency correlates with low earnings and low educational attainment.

There is no consensus as to what constitutes minimum competency; hence there is a wide range of illiteracy estimates. A recent federal government study reported an illiteracy rate among United States adults of 13 percent in 1982, or 17 to 21 million illiterate Americans. On the test used in this study, individuals had to answer twenty out of twenty-six questions correctly to pass. Individuals were asked to "choose the answer that means the same as the word or phrase with an underline under it." Question 1 was:

Persons may receive benefits if they are <u>eligible</u>.
   a. qualified
   b. complete
   c. single
   e. logical

More than one of five individuals with nine to eleven years of education and nearly one in ten high school graduates failed the literacy test. The illiteracy rate among native-born Americans was 9 percent and it was 44 percent among the foreign born.[4] The variation in illiteracy rates among these different groups suggests that efforts to combat illiteracy should concentrate on those without high school diplomas and immigrants.

Employment and earning problems are more likely among those individuals deemed illiterate by the Census Bureau test than among individuals deemed literate. Three of five literate household heads as compared to fewer than two of five illiterate household heads worked year round in 1981. Over one-third of adult illiterates and 13 percent of literate adults had incomes below the poverty line.

Improving the basic skills of workers will increase productivity. Even if a job does not require much reading, a worker's inability to read can be costly. For example, both farmers and janitors need to be able to read the contents listed on chemical containers. In one instance, a herd of cattle had to be destroyed because an illiterate worker unknowingly added a poisonous chemical to its feed.[5]

Work Disabilities

In 1985, one of every twelve individuals between the ages of sixteen and sixty-four suffered from a work disability. Work disabilities impose varying degrees of restriction on an individual. Nearly 7 million adults had a "severe" work disability which impeded their ability to work and they were much more likely to be in poverty than other adults aged sixteen to sixty-four.

	Worked	*In poverty*
Severely disabled	9.4%	44.4%
Disabled, but not severely	69.0	14.1
All adults, aged 16 to 64	77.1	12.1

Even though nearly one in five impoverished adults aged sixteen to sixty-four has a work disability, only a small proportion of the full-time working poor suffer from work disabilities. In 1981, 2.0 million of the 13.1 million disabled adults worked full time year round, including 87,000 who remained in poverty. Almost all disabled workers holding full-time year-round jobs earned reasonable incomes, and their median earnings were only slightly less than that of all workers. Still, disabled full-time year-round workers were almost twice as likely to be found among the working poor than were the nondisabled.[6]

In short, the disabled who can hold full-time year-round jobs are reasonably well off, whereas those whose work ability is either partially or completely limited are highly concentrated in the poverty population. Policies designed to assist the disabled must be targeted to the severity of the disability; a policy of benefit to someone with a nonsevere disability may be of little use to an individual with a severe disability. Distinguishing severe from nonsevere disabilities is not always easy and may not always be consistent. Losing a finger may end a pianist's career but not an economist's.

Second-Chance Programs

The elementary, secondary, and postsecondary education system, along with the home environment, plays a crucial role in teaching youths the skills they require to be effective workers. The education system can bring those on the edge of society into its mainstream and provide a path for upward mobility. Education also provides less tangible but perhaps more important benefits, including a greater understanding of the world around us. For all these reasons, reports in the early 1980s of a deteriorating educational system spurred concern and a rash of proposed reforms.

The educational system is primarily funded and administered by state and local governments. The federal government does, however, play an important role in the system, particularly in supporting the education of the poor from preschool through college. Head Start, perhaps the most universally applauded federal education program, aids the development of preschool children from low-income families; the federal compensatory education system provides aid to students in school districts with a high proportion of low-income families; and college grant and loan programs supply financial assistance to low- and moderate-income students. In addition, the federal government supports the education of the handicapped.

An assessment of the entire educational system lies beyond the scope of this analysis, even though the system has a direct effect on the skill level of workers and thus on the number of working poor.

Table 7. Federal funding for second chance training programs

	Fiscal 1981 (in millions)	Fiscal 1986 (in millions)
Adult and vocational education	$ 728	$1,035
General CETA	3,381	—
JTPA II-A grants to states	—	1,911
Assistance to dislocated workers, JTPA	—	211
Job Corps	540	594
Vocational rehabilitation grants	854	1,145
Total (current dollars)	5,503	4,896
Total (1986 dollars)	6,542	4,896

Source: U.S. Office of Management and Budget

Here the focus is on programs that attempt to assist those who either fail or are failed by the traditional educational system. These programs serve, among others, individuals who lack basic skills and the disabled. "Second-chance" programs will be needed even with an improved educational system. There will always be some individuals who fail to acquire fundamental skills in their childhood and need further assistance.

Second-chance training programs are wide-ranging in design and include adult education programs, basic job training, and vocational rehabilitation programs for the disabled (Table 7). They are intended to lift individuals out of poverty by raising their skill levels.

Basic Education for Adults

The Federal Adult Education Act, first passed in 1966, supports adult basic education (ABE), adult secondary education (ASE), general education development or high school equivalency degrees (GED), and English as a second-language programs (ESL). More than half of all participants are twenty-five years or older. Federal funds are distributed on a formula basis to the states.

In fiscal 1986 the federal government spent $104 million on adult education, and state and local governments contributed twice that amount. Some 2.6 million adults participated in the program, 1.8 million in basic education and .8 million in secondary education. Adult education enrollment increased sharply since Congress passed the 1966 law. In 1984, 281,000 individuals completed the GED.[7] One of five adult education participants is enrolled in an English as second-language program.[8]

The teaching approaches used in adult education programs vary dramatically—one reason why data on their effectiveness are limited. One analysis reported that for every 100 hours of ABE instruction, the average educational gain was .5 grade levels.[9] The teaching of English as a second language has been of particular help to immigrants, many of whom have substantial skills, in finding and retaining employment.

Vocational education programs also help out-of-school individuals acquire job skills. In fiscal 1986 federal government outlays were $931 million and states and localities chipped in eleven times that amount for vocational education. The 1984 Perkins Vocational Education Act emphasizes the needs of adult basic skill training. An estimated 40 percent of vocational education students are twenty-five years or older.[10]

Job Training

As part of the antipoverty efforts of the 1960s, the federal government assumed a major role in training and employing persons with severe labor market problems. A wide range of uncoordinated programs were consolidated in 1973 in the Comprehensive Employment and Training Act (CETA). The Job Training Partnership Act of 1982 (JTPA) superseded CETA.

JTPA differs from CETA in that overall funding has been cut, the public service employment program eliminated, and the role of the private sector emphasized. JTPA places the preponderance of administrative responsibility in the hands of state governors, and the federal government has minimal administrative responsibility. In addition, with few exceptions JTPA provides no stipends and less social service support to participants than did CETA.

Title II-A of JTPA provides training for economically disadvantaged youth and adults. Of the 1.1 million individuals who enrolled in the program in 1985, 790,000 exited the program and 60 percent of them entered the labor force at an average wage of

$4.63 an hour. In 1986 Title II-A funding was $1.9 billion. In early 1987, cost-effectiveness studies of Title II-A were still in the planning stage; however, it is clear that its high placement rate has been partially achieved by selecting the most qualified applicants and providing little assistance to those most in need. In particular, some of those who most need the help cannot get into the programs because they fail the basic skills tests required for admission.

Whether the JTPA local agencies (service delivery areas) deliberately select the most qualified applicants to better their performance results, a practice called "creaming," is one of the most controversial issues surrounding JTPA. Three studies have reported unspecified but widespread creaming. Many service delivery areas tested applicants' reading or math abilities or established minimal educational or occupational skill criteria for admission to JTPA programs. Service providers also screened eligible applicants to select the best qualified.[11]

JTPA emphasizes improved coordination within the many-faceted employment and education system. Eight percent of JTPA funds are set aside to encourage and facilitate cooperation between JTPA training efforts and those of educational institutions. Existing evidence indicates, however, that few improvements in coordination have been made as a result of the legislation.

Title III of JTPA serves dislocated workers who lost their jobs because of plant closings or major layoffs. About one million employees with more than three years' tenure in their jobs are displaced annually because of plant closings or major cutbacks. Program outlays in 1986 amounted to $211 million. Dislocated workers with the least skills and education have the most difficulty finding jobs. The Office of Technology Assessment found that one-fifth of the individuals participating in displaced worker projects need remedial education, but such training is rarely offered.[12]

Job Corps

The Job Corps, which is also funded under JTPA, has achieved a solid record as a successful federal government training program. Established by the Economic Opportunity Act of 1964, the program provides basic education and skill training to disadvantaged out-of-school youth aged fourteen to twenty-one. The program's high cost is due to its comprehensive range of support services and to the location of the training in a residential setting away from the participant's home environment. In fiscal 1986, Job Corps outlays were $594 million. More than a hundred residential training centers were in operation with a total of 40,500 training slots, at an annual cost per slot of $15,000.

The Job Corps serves youth with severe labor market problems who, absent participation, are likely to remain in poverty. Almost three of every four participants are members of minority groups; four of every five have not graduated from high school; and on entry into the program, participants have a median reading level of sixth grade.

Given the difficulty of training and placing disadvantaged youth, the Job Corps' success has been remarkable. A National Research Council review concluded that the Job Corps stood out as an effective training program. It noted that participation in the Job Corps significantly increased employment, earnings, and education, while reducing crime, unemployment compensation, and welfare costs. Benefits accrued not only to the youth who underwent training but also to the general public. Benefits outweighed costs by $2,300 per enrollee (in 1977 dollars).[13]

Bipartisan support for the Job Corps program has ensured its survival despite efforts by the Reagan administration first to eliminate it altogether and, failing that, to cut it back sharply. By improving the skills and work habits of deficiently educated, low-income youth, the Job Corps helps them escape from the ranks of the working poor. The success of the program indicates that with sufficient funding many of the disadvantaged can be helped by federal programs.

Vocational Rehabilitation

The federal government's menu of training programs also includes vocational rehabilitation for the physically and mentally handicapped. Individuals who apply for disability insurance are automatically referred to state vocational rehabilitation agencies. The federal government funds up to 80 percent of the operating costs of these agencies and contributes research, training, and capital grants. In addition to job training, vocational rehabilitation agencies supply a comprehensive list of other services, including medical care and placement. In 1986 an estimated 925,000 individuals were served by these programs, and federal grants to states totaled $1.1 billion.

A 1982 review found that because vocational rehabilitation studies lacked comparison groups, their claimed results should be used with caution. Nevertheless, the investigation concluded that the high benefit-cost ratios indicated a program with positive effects.[14]

An Assessment

Federal second-chance programs are only one small part of the total public-private education and training system. For example, training offered by the Defense Department reaches a significant proportion of low-income youth. Military training may exceed federal outlays for all second-chance teenager programs combined.

The effects of federal second-chance programs are constrained by overall economic trends. In a slack economy, the primary need is not for more skilled workers but to generate greater demand for those workers who are available. In the absence of economic growth, training may only change an individual's place in the queue for jobs, rather than raising the number employed.

The evidence suggests that federal second-chance programs have had a moderately positive effect on the employment prospects of low-income and disadvantaged workers and on diminishing the ranks of the working poor. A wide range of programs corresponding to the differing employment problems of low-income workers seeking assistance is offered. These programs help individuals to acquire basic skills and rehabilitate the disabled. A 1981 comprehensive evaluation estimated that each dollar spent on CETA institutional training resulted in a $1.14 increase in income per participant; the return per dollar of Job Corps training was $1.39.[15] Training has been especially beneficial to adult females.

The Reagan administration, operating on the assumption that the federal government can do relatively little to improve the operation of the labor market, has generally attempted to cut back and even eliminate federal second-chance programs. Such action may generate savings in the short run, but the savings are partially offset by higher welfare expenditures, lower tax revenues, and more unskilled individuals with limited employment opportunities. Advocates of federal second-chance programs argue that they must be continued even in good times to assist those individuals affected by rapid technological change and by intense international economic competition. The views of the proponents have so far prevailed and the federal second-chance employment and training system remains essentially intact, albeit at reduced funding levels.

If a major proportion of those who need assistance are to be served, including some 20 million functionally illiterate adults, the second-chance system requires a much greater investment. Currently, basic education programs assist only the most highly motivated individuals, those who actively seek enrollment. Many more who are reluctant to admit their lack of basic competency tend not to apply. Though some second-chance programs, such as the Job Corps, operate fairly well, others, of course, require modification to enhance their effectiveness. For example, when effective teaching methods for adult education such as computer-assisted training are identified, nationwide application of those methods should be encouraged and funded.

Knocking Down Other Barriers

Inadequate skills and loose labor markets are not the only barriers that prevent the employable poor from obtaining well-paying jobs. Even when jobs are available, women, minorities, and the handicapped can either be locked into low-paying jobs or kept out of jobs altogether because of discrimination. Since the mid-1960s, the federal government has taken the lead in helping to reduce discrimination. The employable poor may also be unable to improve their position because of their inability to provide adequate day care for their children or an inability to overcome other personal problems linked to the struggle against poverty. Adjusted for inflation, federal funding to support day care and related social services needed by the poor to achieve economic self-sufficiency dropped by 17 percent between 1981 and 1986 (Table 8).

Table 8. Federal funding for day care and related social services needed by the poor

	Fiscal 1981 (in millions)	Fiscal 1986 (in millions)
Equal Employment Opportunity Commission	$ 134	$ 162
Social Services Block Grant	2,991	2,671
Head Start	814	1,051
Total (current dollars)	3,939	3,884
Total (1986 dollars)	4,683	3,884

Source: U.S. Office of Management and Budget

Combating Discrimination

Discrimination remains a significant barrier to employment. Although progress toward an equal opportunity society has been made, some employers still fail to hire or promote minorities or women. Both groups are heavily concentrated among the employable poor. The Reagan administration, which viewed the effectiveness of equal employment opportunity programs with skepticism, concentrated much effort on opposing federal affirmative action.

In the 1960s and 1970s, a series of presidential executive orders and federal legislation advanced the cause of equal employment opportunity. The most notable of these, Title VII of the 1964 Civil Rights Act, proscribes discrimination on the basis of race, color, religion, sex, or national origin in hiring, compensation, and promotion. Also, in 1965, President Johnson issued Executive Order 11246 which requires employers doing business with the federal government to document their compliance with equal employment opportunity practices.

The Equal Employment Opportunity Commission (EEOC) administers Title VII. Overt discriminatory practices did decline substantially after the passage of the Civil Rights Act, but institutional discrimination continued. The landmark 1971 Supreme Court decision in *Griggs v. Duke Power Co.* opened the way for

federal enforcement activity directed against institutional discrimination. The Court ruled that Title VII "proscribes not only
overt discrimination but also practices that are fair in form, but
discriminatory in operation." In the 1970s, the use of class action
suits and affirmative action programs further strengthened federal equal employment opportunity efforts.

Many factors affect employment opportunities, making it difficult to isolate the positive effects directly attributable to federal
equal employment activities. Nevertheless, a number of studies
have concluded that the federal equal opportunity drive has contributed to the reduction of wage and employment discrimination.[16] Since the early 1960s, enforcement of civil rights legislation has opened new employment opportunities for minorities and
women. Progress has been limited by shifting economic currents
and by the time lags inherent in providing necessary education
and skills to individuals. Not all the progress is related to government policies, but federal intervention has helped to create an
employment environment conducive to improvement in these areas. Its modest but significant role has been direct in the resolu-
tion of specific cases and it has set an anti-discriminatory tone.
The positive effects may have been greatest for opening upward
mobility opportunities for the targeted groups.

Since 1964, the proportion of blacks employed as managers,
professionals, and craft workers has risen considerably, whereas
the proportion employed in service occupations and as laborers
fell. Women have also experienced employment gains. In 1985,
the proportion of women managers was double that of two decades earlier.

The Reagan administration downgraded the enforcement of
equal employment opportunity policies affecting women and minorities. In 1985, the EEOC was half as successful at achieving
settlements as in 1980 and twice as willing to reject complaints;
but its case backlog was higher.

	1980	1985
Settlement rate	32.1%	14.4%
No-cause rate	28.5%	56.2%
Backlog (thousands)	37.7	44.9

Note: The no-cause rate is the proportion of cases found not worthy of
litigating by the EEOC.

In contrast to federal practice in the 1970s, the Reagan administration emphasized cases involving individual victims of discrimination; class action suits were discouraged. The administration
sharply attacked affirmative action—the use of goals and numeri-
cal approaches to combat discrimination. The administration has
been embroiled in controversy over the Justice Department's de-
sire (over the Labor Department's opposition) to alter Executive
Order 11246, the federal government's most important affirmative action tool. The Justice Department also supported disman-
tling specific affirmative action plans in federal court actions.

The actions of the Reagan administration slowed progress on
the equal employment opportunity front. Lax enforcement resulted in less direct relief to the victims of discrimination and
sent a signal to employers that combating discrimination was no
longer a national priority, and perhaps led some businesses to
revert to old practices. In response to political and court pressure,
however, the administration did modify its opposition to class-
based relief and affirmative action. Civil rights proponents prevented significant change in equal employment opportunity stat-
utes and blocked the appointment of some officials who were
opposed to federal equal employment opportunity efforts. The Supreme Court rejected the attempts of the Justice Department to
overturn voluntary affirmative action agreements. In a series of
decisions in mid-1986, the Court upheld the use of affirmative
action to overcome discrimination.[17]

The federal government also helps promote the equal treatment
of the handicapped in employment and education, although the
effects of these efforts remain to be determined. The Rehabilitation Act of 1973, for example, requires the federal government to
submit an affirmative action program for the employment of the
handicapped and prohibits companies doing business with the
federal government from discriminating against the handicapped.

Social Services and Day Care

Goals of federal social service programs include helping poor
families achieve economic self-support, preventing the neglect of
children, and helping to secure institutional care. These efforts

can assist a poor family in providing care for its children, in dealing with emotional problems, and in finding a job.

The Omnibus Budget Reconciliation Act consolidated federal funding of social services (Title XX of the Social Security Act) into a block grant, distributed to states based on population. The 1981 act gave the states flexibility in allocating the grant; for example, states no longer must supply matching funds and do not have to adhere to federal income eligibility standards. The size of the social services program has decreased considerably in the 1980s. In fiscal 1986, the entitlement ceiling was $2.7 billion, a reduction of 25 percent in just five years after adjusting for inflation.

The service most commonly provided by these block grants is day care. More than half of all women heads of household with a child under six years old worked in 1985. The provision of affordable, adequate day care is essential for the working poor. It enables a poor mother to work without endangering the health and well-being of her children.

Before the 1981 amendments to the Social Security Act, more than one-fifth of total social services funding was allocated to child care. There were also federal standards regulating the operation of social service day care centers. Currently, the states determine how much of their block grant goes to day care and establish their own standards for these facilities. According to the Children's Defense Fund, in 1981, Title XX served 472,000 of the 3.4 million impoverished children under six years old. By 1985, there were 4.9 million children in the same age bracket, but there was less money available under Title XX.[18]

Head Start is the most effective child care and development program for impoverished children. The program provides a comprehensive range of services to 452,000 preschool children, and had a price tag of $1.1 billion in fiscal 1986. This approach has been successful in helping children of the poor overcome their background deficiencies. Longitudinal studies have found that Head Start participants are more likely to graduate from high school, enroll in college, and obtain a self-supporting job than nonparticipants with similar backgrounds.[19] The program's success highlights the importance of a nurturing environment for the young and the wisdom of federal efforts to assist poor children. As an answer to the day care problems of the working poor, however, Head Start is limited. Its funding is low relative to the potential number of participants. In most cases, Head Start provides care for only four to six hours a day, and thus the children of full-time workers are excluded. The cost per participant would be sharply increased if Head Start served as a provider of child care for impoverished families with full-time working mothers.

Other federal programs, including Aid to Families with Dependent Children and the Work Incentive Program, also promote and provide child care funding. Together, however, the wide range of federal programs providing child care assistance fails to reach many low-wage parents. A woman who works at the minimum wage and earns $7,000 a year can scarcely afford even low-cost day care. Consequently, poor working mothers are forced to cope with inadequate care for their young children and many older children return from school to empty homes.

The child care tax credit provides substantial indirect federal funding for child care. In 1986 it amounted to a revenue loss of an estimated $3.2 billion. Even though the program provides the largest tax credit (30 percent) to low-income individuals, the program primarily benefits middle- and upper-income families.[20] The tax credit is of little help to poor parents with limited federal income tax liability who are not able to afford the up-front costs of day care. The tax credit would be of greater benefit to the working poor if it were refundable.

Reforms

The basic structure of existing equal employment opportunity law is sound; the limits to its effectiveness lie in the lack of adequate and vigorous enforcement. The commitment to promoting equal employment opportunity could be affirmed by reduction of the EEOC case backlog, by active use of affirmative action programs and by resorting to class-based relief when appropriate. Through the oversight process, Congress could promote the adequate enforcement of equal employment opportunity laws. A comprehensive social service program would require added outlays that could be used exclusively for day care support for low-income families with workers.

Are the Walls Crumbling Down?

A significant number of adult Americans lack the basic educational and vocational skills necessary for productive and well-paying employment. The key to assisting these individuals lies in strengthening both the basic and second-chance education systems. Those who pass through the system without acquiring basic skills are likely to have low incomes, to be subject to intermittent spells of forced unemployment, and to become dependent on welfare. Federal second-chance opportunities fill a gap in the education and training system. The best of these programs offer a well-targeted approach to the problems of the employable poor.

Attainment of basic skill competency alone is not sufficient to enable many of the poor to obtain sustained employment, even in an expanding economy. There is also a need for enforcement of equal employment opportunity laws and for subsidized inexpensive day care. The federal government has provided day care for only a small proportion of children in poverty.

The emphasis here on federal policies should not obscure the need for business, unions, and state and local governments to work toward removing barriers to employment. Employers can provide skill training and voluntarily promote equal employment opportunity. States and localities, which administer most of the federal second-chance programs, have primary responsibility for the funding and quality of the education system. In addition, although the working poor are often victims, their own participation and responsibility for improving their lot is crucial. Many are failed by the school system and the labor markets, but others fail school or lack the self-discipline and motivation to find a niche in the workplace. A combined and concerted effort on the part of all involved could improve workers' basic skills and lower other barriers to employment.

6. Finding and Creating Jobs

Complementing efforts to knock down employment barriers, the federal government plays a direct role in improving the functioning of the labor market and in generating demand for workers. Several programs assist the employable poor when they are seeking work. Many jobs remain vacant because institutions designed to match job openings with those seeking work are inadequate. Though the United States economy has been successful in generating new jobs, it has not created enough demand to employ all workers.

The federal-state employment service (also known as the job service) attempts to match available workers with vacant jobs. The service is federally funded through the unemployment insurance trust fund and is state administered (within broad federal guidelines). Through counseling and testing of workers, it expedites the filling of jobs to the benefit of both employers and the new employees.

Federal policies also offer employers special inducements to hire poor youth, welfare recipients, and other economically disadvantaged individuals. Subsidies compensate employers for the extra efforts required to train unskilled employees with poor work records. Currently, the federal subsidy to employers is in the form of a tax credit which encourages the hiring of disadvantaged workers.

The job service and tax credit programs fail to reach many targeted workers who remain unemployed even in an expanding economy. In an effort to employ idle workers, the federal government funded major public service employment programs during the 1930s and again in the 1970s. Although the largest public service employment program was eliminated in 1981, the federal government still funds summer jobs for hundreds of thousands of poor youngsters, part-time employment for the low-income elderly, and sheltered workshops which provide a combination of employment and training for the handicapped.

The Employment Service

Filling job vacancies expeditiously and inexpensively benefits employers and potential employees alike. Employers reap savings when production interruptions are reduced and employees benefit from increased income as well as from shorter job searches. Moreover, society as a whole benefits when the unemployed become taxpayers.

In the dynamic United States economy, many jobs remain vacant even if qualified individuals are looking for work. Private-sector mechanisms, such as employment agencies, do facilitate the job-matching process, but they serve mostly workers who can afford the services or employers who are willing to pay employment agencies to find qualified workers. The poor are unable to pay for job-search assistance and for-profit employment agencies typically do not list jobs for the unskilled. A formal and free job-matching system is of vital assistance to low-wage and unskilled workers.

Background

The Wagner-Peyser Act of 1933 established a national network of federally financed state-run employment services to match workers with jobs and to refer the unemployed to other available support services. Because the employment service was charged with the responsibility to administer the availability-for-work test (a condition for receiving unemployment benefits), the service acquired its enduring image as an *unemployment* office as opposed to a *placement* office. In the 1960s, the employment service focused on assistance to disadvantaged workers rather than acting as a labor exchange for job seekers. In the 1970s, the service emphasized development of job listings. The Job Training Partnership Act of 1982 gave the states more discretionary authority to administer the service. The act supported improved coordination between the service and the rest of the employment and training system and encouraged business involvement in program planning.

The employment service as currently constituted has a wide range of sometimes conflicting missions. It is a labor exchange which attempts to serve all workers seeking jobs and employers, but Congress has mandated that its assistance be targeted to veterans, youth, the handicapped, and the economically disadvantaged. Moreover, in addition to its functions of job matching, collecting and analyzing labor market data, and administering the unemployment insurance work test, the job service has been given responsibility for registering food stamp and AFDC recipients, and certifying foreign workers for employment. Notwithstanding its broad functions and responsibilities, job service staff levels declined by one-third from 1980 to 1984. Federal expenditures for basic labor exchange services, funded by the federal payroll tax on employers, totaled $769 million in 1986.

Services Provided

Because of its limited funding and its wide-ranging responsibilities, the employment service does not operate so much as an active placement office but more as a passive matcher of job openings with job seekers. The service collects information from job applicants and refers applicants to employers.

The employment service fills about 7 to 8 percent of all job openings. In 1984 one-fourth of the 15 million employment service applicants were placed in jobs (some more than once). A much smaller percentage of applicants were tested or counseled.

New and renewal applicants	15,083,000
Individuals placed	3,548,000
Percent placed	23.5
Percent tested	4.0
Percent counseled	4.0

Although the employment service's record relative to the number of applicants and the overall number of job openings is not impressive, it does help millions of workers find jobs each year. It primarily benefits low-skilled and unemployed job seekers. Twenty-five to 30 percent of employment service applicants are economically disadvantaged and 5 percent are handicapped. A General Accounting Office study in the early 1980s found that employment service clients tend to be younger and less educated than the overall labor force.[1]

The jobs found through the employment service are often low paying and short term. In 1981, over half of these jobs paid between $3.10 and $3.99 an hour ($3.35 was the prevailing minimum wage), and 40 percent were expected to last less than five months. Such jobs generally offered little opportunity for upward mobility.[2]

Effectiveness

The effectiveness of the employment service has been subject to little rigorous assessment. One exception is a comprehensive analysis of the agency's operation from mid-1980 to mid-1981. This study found that women referred to jobs by employment service offices experienced gains in income whereas men who received such services had no identifiable gains. These benefits were shown to exceed the costs of the program by a factor of two to one.[3] Charges about the low quality of employment service referrals are commonplace, but employers listed 7.4 million jobs with the service in 1984, indicating a fair degree of satisfaction with the service.

In the 1980s, the federal government has essentially abdicated its oversight responsibility for the operations of the employment service. The national staff that reviews employment service plans and activities has been cut from over 100 to less than 20. The lack of oversight is likely to exacerbate the already substantial variation in the effectiveness of employment service agencies in different states and localities. Employment service policies should be tailored to local needs, but this tailoring does not obviate the need for minimal federal standards and the collection and centralization of information on effective approaches.

Reforms

Observers agree that the employment service's effectiveness would be enhanced if its mission were clarified. The service handles a wide diversity of tasks and would benefit from a period of stability. If its role were clarified and refined, and some of its more extraneous responsibilities eliminated, the service's functioning might well improve.

A perennial controversy exists over whether the employment service should target its services primarily to the disadvantaged. The unemployed use a variety of methods in their job hunts, ranging from reliance on personal contacts, to response to advertisements, to the use of private and public employment agencies. Only about one in thirteen job seekers finds employment through the public employment service and the number of private agencies has grown sharply in the last ten years. Should the public employment service compete with private employment agencies, coordinate with these agencies, or pursue a separate market niche?

If the employment service improves the quality of its job listings and its applicants, its reputation will be enhanced, but its service to the disadvantaged may suffer. On the other hand, if it continues to serve mostly low-skilled workers, the job vacancies that employers report to the agency will continue to be of low quality.

There are other possibilities for improving the employment service. Experiments in which the employment service referred some of its applicants to private agencies indicate that this approach might benefit applicants.[4] Increased funding would make it possible for states to strengthen their job development and outreach efforts. The substitution of standardized tests for interviews could improve the screening process and the use of new data processing techniques would improve overall functioning.

Sharp criticism of the employment service may arise in part from unrealistic expectations. Most individuals find jobs through informal networks rather than institutional arrangements. An appropriate measure of the employment service's utility is whether it plays a beneficial role, however limited, in helping to facilitate the job search of millions of Americans each year. The employment service passes this test. As long as there are employers who search for workers in a haphazard fashion, and as long as there are employees who are unable to find suitable jobs on their own, the employment service will be needed to bring them together.

Targeted Jobs Tax Credit

Wage subsidies fit neatly into the classic economic equation—to increase the demand for goods, lower their price. Wage subsidies are based on the premise that they compensate employers for the lower productivity associated with unskilled workers. Government wage subsidies thus theoretically provide employers with incentive to hire eligible workers. In contrast to welfare expenditures, moreover, wage subsidies help the poor obtain secure and lasting employment. Also, wage subsidies increase employer demand for workers without lowering wages.[5]

The theoretical appeal of government wage subsidies has not been borne out by the adoption of an effective wage subsidy system. Designing an effective wage subsidy system is no easy task. It is difficult to ensure that employers do not reap a windfall by receiving a subsidy for employees they would have hired anyway. There is also a danger that subsidized workers may be substituted for unsubsidized workers. The limited subsidy experiments to date have shown the unexpected difficulty of attracting employers to their plans, suggesting that other factors—workers' lack of skills or low demand for products or employer bias—influence hiring decisions more than wage barriers.

Since 1978, the targeted jobs tax credit (TJTC) has been the major federal wage subsidy program. Because of problems in program design and the failure of federal monitoring, TJTC can hardly be called a success. Nevertheless, if the program were properly modified and employer participation increased, it would be an important part of federal policy options designed to assist the employable poor. The 1986 tax reform law failed to take the necessary steps that would make TJTC more effective.

How TJTC Works

TJTC offers a tax credit to employers who hire targeted individuals. The credit amounts to 40 percent of the first $6,000 paid during the initial year of employment. For disadvantaged youth aged sixteen to seventeen years who are hired for a summer job, the credit amounts to 85 percent of up to $3,000.

TJTC benefits low-income youth and young adults aged sixteen to twenty-four years, impoverished Vietnam era veterans, handicapped individuals receiving vocational rehabilitation, and AFDC or general assistance recipients. Altogether, about 7 million individuals are potentially eligible for TJTC. Most unemployed poor adults, however, do not qualify for TJTC. Over the years, the number of individuals certified for program participa-

Figure 8. Youth account for a majority of TJTC certifications, 1985.

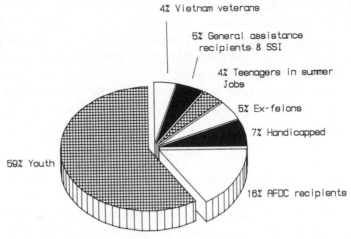

Source: U.S. Department of Labor

tion has continued to rise, except during the recession year of 1982. In 1985, a total of 622,000 individuals were certified to participate in the program, well over half of whom were youths (Figure 8).

An individual, an employer, or a government agency (usually the public employment office) can initiate a TJTC eligibility determination. Job seekers are screened by the local employment service, job training, public assistance, or vocational rehabilitation office, and vouchers are issued to eligible applicants. Employers can request a referral of TJTC-eligible job seekers from the local employment service office or can ask the office to review the TJTC eligibility of applicants or the newly hired.

Only ballpark estimates of the cost of TJTC are available; no tally of the credits taken by employers is compiled. The Office of Management and Budget estimated that the 1986 revenue loss from TJTC was $510 million, but this figure was based on limited data.

More Jobs or Employer Windfalls?

Although 2.6 million workers were certified under the TJTC during its first six years of operation, it is difficult to determine whether the program increased either the hiring of the target population or total employment. The lack of basic information about TJTC's operations and results compounds the always difficult task of evaluation. Available data indicate that the program needs substantial reform before it will be fully effective.

Despite the tax credit, employers have shown considerable reluctance to hire TJTC eligibles. A 1982 government survey found that three of four employers indicated lack of interest in the program. Employers who perceived targeted individuals as unproductive had little confidence that public employment offices would refer acceptable applicants.[6] The accuracy of this survey is in doubt, however, because it included firms that did not employ low-skilled workers. Those employers who did hire targeted workers believed them to be about as productive as other employees in the same occupation. Overall, the survey found that even when employers became familiar with the potential benefits of employing TJTC eligibles, they still hesitated to participate in the program.

Three studies have examined whether holding a TJTC voucher improves the employment prospects of targeted individuals. Two demonstration projects, one by the federal government and one by the State of Wisconsin, concluded that vouchered jobs applicants were less likely to be hired than comparable nonvouchered applicants.[7] These results have led to claims that tax credits are counterproductive because vouchered job seekers are stigmatized. If the study results are confirmed, other means of marketing job tax credits should be investigated. For example, the employment service could identify employers who have indicated a willingness to participate in the program and suggest to individuals with TJTC vouchers to contact these firms.

A third study, conducted at Ohio State University, concluded that the impact of vouchers was partially dependent on the qualifications of the applicant. In a hypothetical test, employers viewed low-skilled TJTC applicants more favorably than those with more education or job experience. The authors of this study speculated that, though individuals qualified for more than entry level jobs might be stigmatized by a TJTC voucher, lower-skilled individuals benefit from the program.[8]

Other labor market effects of TJTC are also uncertain. The

limited available evidence shows that the average earnings of TJTC workers is close to the minimum wage. A study of one small sample found that in 1981 the average employment duration of TJTC workers was only 3.5 months.[9]

Whatever the impact of TJTC on job search success, employers have generated the bulk of TJTC eligibility requests. Many employers who would have hired the same individuals in the absence of the TJTC (and in some cases had already hired them) took advantage of the TJTC to collect the subsidy. Although the law requires that employers must apply for TJTC eligibility determinations before an employee begins work, this provision has been at best only partially successful in preventing windfall benefits to employers. Requests for certification of all the newly hired can be made merely by submitting their names to the local public employment office on or before the date they begin work.

When TJTC eligibility requests are made after hiring, the program's objective—to increase employment opportunities for targeted individuals who otherwise might not be hired—is obviously not achieved. The growing practice of businesses to hire intermediaries to process claims for subsidies with public employment offices fuels this concern. These intermediaries primarily secure post-hiring vouchers. In a survey of twelve states, employment service officials of five states estimated that these consultants generated more than 50 percent of TJTC vouchers.[10] Another study found that some employers forward the names of *all* the newly hired to intermediaries, who then present letters of request to the public employment office.[11] The extent of post-hire vouchers on a national basis is unknown. A Maryland study found that, between 1982 and 1985, post-hiring requests accounted for about two of five TJTC certifications.[12]

Strengthening the Program

One potential TJTC reform would involve federal monitoring and information dissemination. Without reliable estimates on the costs of TJTC, the extent of post-hiring certifications, and the nature of the jobs created, it is difficult to assess the program's effectiveness and to decide what reforms might be most helpful. Evidence from the two studies suggesting that TJTC vouchers stigmatize job seekers, though preliminary, is troubling to TJTC advocates. Further experiments could help assess the impact of TJTC certification on job search.

The problem presented by employers who obtain tax credits for employees who would have been hired anyway or have already been hired could be addressed by requiring employers, subject to appropriate penalties, to certify that these applicants were hired after the voucher request. If the employment service were strengthened, it could exercise more effective oversight of TJTC claims. In addition, it could improve its referrals, thus decreasing the stigma associated with the use of TJTC.

In the past, most TJTC hires were employed at poverty wages in temporary jobs. Raising the wage base that TJTC is applicable to, while lowering the tax credit from its current 40 percent, would provide employers added incentive to offer higher-paying longer-lasting jobs. Lengthening the required duration of employment (currently 120 hours or 90 days) or establishing a minimum amount of wages to be paid before employers become eligible for a tax credit would save tax expenditures and prevent unjustified tax claims. Of course, TJTC would do more for the working poor if eligibility were extended to all low-income workers, but such an expansion may be appropriate only after the federal budget deficit declines and after program deficiencies are corrected.

The verdict is still out on the effectiveness of wage subsidies as a vehicle for encouraging employers to hire the poor and other groups that need assistance to compete in the labor market. Little has been learned from the eight years of the TJTC program because the departments of Labor and Treasury failed to monitor and evaluate the program and Congress neglected its oversight responsibilities. The fragmentary available data indicate that the majority of the program's beneficiaries are low-income youth. The design of the program prevents it from being of much assistance to the adult working poor. TJTC may be an experiment worth continuing, but only if the reforms necessary to improve its operation are made.

Job Creation

Wage subsidies and facilitation of the job-matching process are market-based approaches designed to help individuals with employment problems. However, these programs are of little assistance to the unemployed if jobs are not available. Federally funded public service jobs perform a countercyclical role; they can provide employment opportunities during periods of slack economic demand, and they can also help individuals whose employment problems persist during periods of economic growth and expansion.

Forsaken Too Soon?

The first and largest federal public service employment effort was created as a response to the Great Depression. New Deal programs were based on the belief that the federal government could and should play an active role as an antidote to mass unemployment and the widespread deprivation then prevailing. The Work Projects Administration, the largest New Deal job creation program, employed more than 3 million workers at its peak in 1936.[13] WPA workers built airposts, thousands of libraries, and developed public parks.[14]

After World War II the economy expanded and public job creation programs came into disfavor. It was not until the 1960s, when it was recognized that the employment problems of the economically disadvantaged continued even during periods of low unemployment, that public service employment once again became a federal policy tool. Public job creation efforts were on a relatively small scale in the 1960s. In contrast, in the 1970s the federal government spent billions of dollars on job creation. The last expansion was in 1977 when the public service employment program increased from 300,000 to 750,000 job slots.[15] The program was curtailed in 1979 and terminated two years later.

What factors contributed to the demise of the public service employment program? It was perceived as inefficient, as providing make-work jobs and as being subject to abuse and manipulation by local authorities. In addition, it was ineffective as a countercyclical tool; by the time a program passed Congress and was implemented, economic recovery had begun. When the Reagan administration, consistent with its advocacy of curbing federal intervention in the economy, proposed elimination of the program, Congress went along with little opposition.

A closer look at the operations of public service employment might have convinced Congress that the program was worth saving. Local abuse was less common than generally believed, and public service employment can be beneficial both to participants and society. Constant revision of the program led to conflicting objectives and expectations. Public service jobs can be implemented in a more timely fashion by instituting a permanent program with an automatic provision to trigger expansion during recessions and contraction during recoveries. CETA provided for such an approach, but the Ford and Carter administrations ignored this provision.

The value of public service employment (PSE) depends both on the number and nature of the jobs created. Critics have charged that the jobs created by federally funded programs substitute for jobs that localities would have funded in the absence of such federal assistance. One study of public service employment from 1977 to 1980 found otherwise, estimating that 80 to 90 percent of PSE funding contributed to job creation as opposed to job displacement. This same study found that valuable services were provided to individuals and communities through these jobs, including library services, "meals on wheels," park renovation, and road repair.[16] Society benefited from the productive output of the employees and from the reduction in public welfare expenditures. Public service job programs are also in accord with the prevailing notion that individuals should work in return for public assistance.

Ongoing Programs

The summer youth employment program (Title II-B of JTPA) is targeted to economically disadvantaged youths aged sixteen to twenty-one years old. These youths are hired at the minimum wage and given a chance to gain work experience. There is some evidence that participants have been more likely to stay in school and less likely to be arrested.[17] Although the low-income youths served by this program are especially in need of public service employment, its funding was cut in the 1980s from $839 million in the summer of 1981 to $746 million in the summer of 1986, a reduction of almost 30 percent after adjusting for inflation.

The Community Service Employment Program for Older Americans funds part-time employment at or slightly above the minimum wage for low-income individuals aged fifty-five and over. These jobs provide a variety of community services directed to the needs of the elderly. In 1986, federal funding for this program was $321 million, providing part-time employment to about 100,000 individuals, representing only a small fraction of the nation's eligible elderly.[18]

The federal government provides vocational rehabilitation assistance through sheltered workshops, most of which are run by private, nonprofit agencies. Sheltered workshops provide temporary employment and training for the moderately disabled and more permanent employment for the severely disabled. Work capacity among the disabled varies widely, and sheltered workshops have been most cost effective for those with only moderate disabilities. Programs for the severely disabled, in which costs are high and productivity is low, are valuable more in terms of the sociopsychological benefits of work.[19] In 1984 one-quarter million handicapped workers were certified to work in sheltered workshops. The certification allows employers to pay disabled workers less than the minimum wage, which sometimes results in extremely low compensation. Of those certified, three out of four were employed in work activities centers that assist handicapped individuals with limited productive capacities.

Revival

Throughout the 1970s, the administration of public service employment programs improved. Congress tightened eligibility standards and cut the duration of public service jobs to minimize substitution. These amendments had their costs, however. Individuals without basic skills would have been far better served by intensive training than by public service jobs. In addition, political support for the program eroded. Localities were less interested in employment of low-skilled individuals on temporary projects than in hiring better-skilled workers for longer durations. Public service employment, however, not only is more precisely targeted than tax incentives, but it can provide an appropriate supplement to existing employment opportunities. Federal assistance can help the unemployed in those states and localities which have the highest unemployment rates and which lack the financial resources to create jobs on their own.

Not Much Help

In the 1980s Congress sharply curtailed, with strong lobbying from the Reagan administration, the modest federal employment service and job creation programs. Though the employment service places millions of workers each year, there is widespread agreement that it needs considerable reform and strengthening. The Targeted Jobs Tax Credit program has been in effect for nine years but has provided questionable help to the employable poor. The largest public service jobs program, which funded jobs for about one of every ten unemployed persons in 1977, was eliminated in 1981. Most workers will continue to find jobs without federal assistance, but the federal government has a significant role to play in helping the disadvantaged find employment.

7. Linking Welfare with Work

Earlier chapters examined various policies that promote economic self-sufficiency by raising the earnings of low-paid workers, funding skill-training programs, helping the unemployed find jobs and creating jobs for those who seek but cannot find work. These efforts are the most preferable approach to addressing the problems of the working poor. It is sounder public policy to assist the poor in attaining economic self-sufficiency than to have them depend on welfare payments: society benefits both from the increased output of the working poor and from lower welfare costs. The goal of public policy should be to generate enough jobs so that all who can work are able to escape poverty, thus leaving only the unemployable to rely on welfare assistance.

Equating employment with economic self-sufficiency, free market advocates argue that any adult who has a job does not need welfare assistance. The poverty status of the working poor negates this assertion. Disqualifying the working poor from welfare assistance will discourage work effort if welfare is more rewarding than work. For example, a low-income parent's need for affordable medical care may be sufficiently compelling to lead that individual to forsake work in order to qualify for medicaid. Welfare may be a last resort, but it is a necessary one if the working poor and their families are to obtain the basic necessities of life in the continued absence of adequate wages.

The welfare and social insurance system works in a perverse way and is often of scant help to the working poor. Cash assistance to the working poor is negligible. In-kind benefits provide some aid, but most working poor are denied these benefits. Many of the working poor do not have health insurance and are ineligible for medicaid assistance. Social insurance programs benefit low-income individuals when they retire, become disabled, or lose their jobs, but not when they are working. Welfare assistance to the working poor has declined in the 1980s both because of overall cuts in domestic programs and because specific cuts have reduced aid to the working poor.

This chapter also examines the mounting interest in work programs for welfare recipients. The growing controversy in this area has been driven by the Reagan administration's promotion of mandatory workfare and nourished by the beliefs that work improves the long-term prospects of the recipients and that the right to welfare assistance engenders a responsibility to society.

The debate over work incentives and work requirements for welfare recipients has deflected attention away from the welfare system's inadequacy in addressing the needs of the working poor. The system's failure clearly limits the rewards attainable through work. The working poor should be eligible to receive welfare and social insurance assistance as a necessary complement to their meager earnings; for them, work and welfare must go together. It is inconsistent for conservatives to disdain efforts to improve the working conditions of low-wage employees and at the same time support cuts in welfare benefits.

Cash Assistance

Aid to Families with Dependent Children (AFDC) is the largest means-tested cash benefit program. It provides assistance to impoverished families, most of whom are headed by females. About two-thirds of AFDC recipients are children and, in nine out of ten AFDC families, the father is absent. The federal government finances more than half of AFDC costs, but individual states establish need and benefit standards and administer the program. Families constantly move on and off AFDC rolls (about one-half of AFDC beneficiaries receive aid for two years or less), but a majority of those receiving AFDC benefits at any time are subject to long poverty spells. Many individuals dip into poverty temporarily, but a hard-core group absorbs the bulk of AFDC expenditures.[1]

In fiscal 1986 federal and state AFDC outlays totaled $17.7 billion and benefited a monthly average of 11.1 million individuals. Total expenditures adjusted for inflation grew dramatically until 1973, stabilized through 1977, contracted, and then once again stabilized in 1982. Though the number of recipients has remained relatively constant since 1972, the average monthly benefit level per family, after adjusting for inflation, fell 31 percent from 1970 to 1985. Since the number of dependents per family also declined during that period, the average monthly payment per recipient dropped by only 9 percent.

AFDC payments leave most families in poverty. For a family of three living in a state with median AFDC support, the maximum AFDC grant combined with food stamp benefits yields less than three-quarters of the poverty-income threshold. The maximum AFDC grant varies substantially among states, but AFDC support and food stamps raise a family of three above poverty only in Alaska and Suffolk County, New York.

The AFDC program is especially skimpy when it comes to providing benefits to the working poor. In half of the states, two-parent households are excluded from receiving AFDC support. States that provide AFDC to two-parent families in which the principal earner is unemployed (AFDC-UP) include, however, most of the relatively high-benefit states and about 71 percent of the total AFDC caseload. In all states, federal law proscribes the payment of AFDC-UP benefits to impoverished families with full-time workers.

The Omnibus Budget Reconciliation Act of 1981 (OBRA) substantially lowered AFDC benefits for families with earned income. Among other limiting provisions, OBRA changed the basis of calculating the amount of earnings that was excluded in calculating the level of AFDC benefits—the $30 and one-third earned income disregard—from net to gross income. The impact of this change was to raise the earnings that determine the cash assistance to the working poor, thus decreasing their benefits. OBRA restricted the use of the earned income disregard from a year to only four consecutive months of employment. Earnings after the first four months could no longer be partially disregarded in calculating benefits. OBRA also restricted benefits to families with gross income equal to 150 percent of the state need standard and placed a cap of $75 on work-expense deductions for full-time employment.

The effects of this legislation on the working poor were immediate and dramatic. The General Accounting Office found that OBRA led to a drop in monthly AFDC caseloads of 442,000 and a decline in monthly payments of $92.8 million.[2] A survey of five sites found that, six months after OBRA took effect, 66 to 87 percent of AFDC families with earnings had their cash benefits reduced or eliminated. Some of the benefit reductions were due to earnings increases, but about two-thirds of these changes were due to OBRA. By 1983, only 6 percent of AFDC families, compared with 13 percent in 1979, had earnings (Figure 9).

Figure 9. Legislative changes in 1981 reduced the number of AFDC recipients who have earned income.

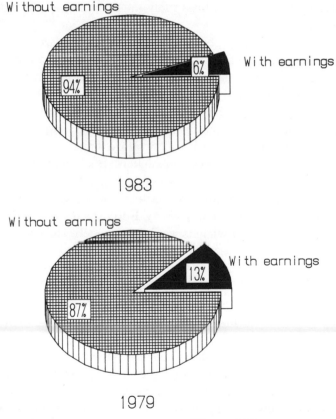

Source: U.S. Congress, House Committee on Ways and Means

The working poor receive only limited assistance from other cash support programs. The General Accounting Office found that 95 percent of those individuals who were dropped from the AFDC rolls were ineligible for income-support programs such as the small state general assistance programs. The cutback in AFDC assistance resulted in an inadequate food supply and lack of medical care for many benefit losers. Families disqualified from AFDC support lost their automatic eligibility for medicaid. These income and benefit losses from AFDC were not recouped through increased earnings.

Congress subsequently relaxed some of OBRA's harsher provisions, raising AFDC earnings and gross income limits and allowing some individuals dropped from the AFDC rolls to qualify for medicaid. Still, AFDC is less generous to families with earnings than it was before 1981. Less than one-fifth of the 1981 cuts were restored.[3]

Extending AFDC eligibility to all impoverished two-parent families would eliminate the incentive for families to break up in order to qualify for cash assistance. If the ninety-nine-hour-per-month work limit were lifted, two-parent families with a full-time worker at low wages might be eligible for AFDC-UP benefits. These changes would reflect the reality that the working poor need income assistance, that work and welfare have to go together to eliminate poverty for low-wage workers. Such changes would expand the scope of AFDC beyond female-headed households without earnings to both one- and two-parent households with earnings that nevertheless remain in poverty. Fully restoring the pre-OBRA earnings disregard provisions would also benefit the working poor.

In-Kind Benefits

The major means-tested in-kind benefit programs include food stamps, medical care, and housing assistance. Real spending for these programs has increased dramatically since the mid-1960s, but in 1984 only one in three poor households in which the head worked for part or all of the year received food stamps, one in four received medicaid, and one in ten received housing assistance. A higher percentage of the nonworking poor receive the same benefits. In 1984 half of all nonworking poor households received food stamps, 55 percent received medicaid, and one in five received housing assistance. The proportion of working poor who received in-kind assistance stabilized in the 1980s (Figure 10).

The food stamp program is funded almost entirely by the federal government. Benefit standards are applied nationally, and state welfare agencies administer the program. The program has few categorical restrictions. A low-income household is eligible to participate even if there are two parents, one of whom works full time. A recipient's benefits are equal to the maximum benefit level reduced by 30 percent of the household's net income (after certain allowable deductions). The income limits are high enough to include most impoverished workers, but stringent liquid asset limits equal to $2,000—excluding the value of a residence, a portion of the value of motor vehicles, and certain other resources—preclude some of the working poor from receiving benefits even if they qualify on the basis of income.

Figure 10. A smaller proportion of the working poor than the nonworking poor receive in-kind benefits, 1984.

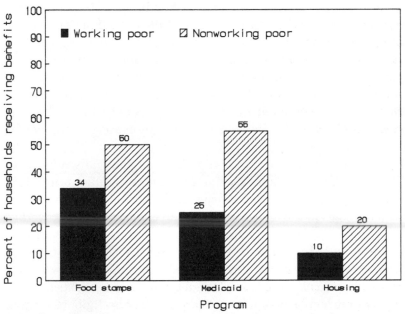

Source: U.S. Bureau of the Census

The food stamp program benefits about 21.3 million individuals with a 1986 price tag of $12.6 billion. The average monthly value per person is equal to $45. For a four-person family, the maximum monthly gross income eligibility limit is $1,154 and the maximum monthly benefit level is $268. The food stamp allotment is designed to enable a family to maintain what the Department of Agriculture calls a "nutritionally adequate" diet, but this regimen requires sophisticated nutritional planning skills, refrigerated storage space, equipment, and low-cost markets—all resources frequently unavailable to the poor. Agriculture Department surveys have found that nine in ten families with food expenditures equal to the maximum food stamp level have inadequate diets. Roughly 10 million individuals who are eligible for food stamps do not receive them.[4] Many do not apply because they would qualify for limited assistance, lack information about the program or because of the stigma involved in receiving food stamps.

Federal government medical assistance programs include medicare which provides aid to the elderly, regardless of their income, whereas medicaid serves primarily the indigent, elderly, disabled, and other nonworking poor. In 1986, total outlays for medicaid amounted to $44.7 billion, and 22.6 million individuals were served. The federal government contributed $25.0 billion and the states contributed the balance, making medicaid the costliest means-tested benefit program. The states, subject to federal guidelines, have substantial discretion in program administration. Low-income aged and disabled account for almost three-quarters of all medicaid payments and AFDC recipients receive most of the remaining benefits. All three groups are automatically eligible for medicaid.

The working poor who receive AFDC automatically qualify for medicaid benefits, and special provisions qualify other low-earnings families for limited specified assistance. For example, 1986 changes in the law enable states to extend medicaid coverage to *all* impoverished pregnant women and, eventually, to all poor children up to five years old. In 1984 only 13 percent of impoverished households whose head worked full time, forty weeks or more, had one or more family members covered by medicaid. Under current regulations, a family or individual is eligible for either the entire package of medicaid benefits or for none. There is no sliding benefits scale.

Not only are the bulk of the working poor excluded from medicaid coverage, but only a few receive health insurance from their jobs. Two-thirds of impoverished household heads who worked full time, forty weeks or more, in 1984 were not covered by employer- or union-subsidized health insurance plans. Even fewer part-time poor workers were covered under such plans. The working poor who are fortunate enough to have group health coverage, as compared to higher paid workers, are likely to pay proportionately more of their wages for less adequate coverage.[5]

Because the eligibility requirements for public housing and rent supplements are income based, the working poor are eligible to receive housing assistance under these two federal programs. However, only one in ten of the working poor live in publicly owned or subsidized private rental housing. Two in ten nonworking poor households receive such assistance.

Legislative changes in the 1980s reduced federal housing assistance to low-income families. The construction of new public housing units has almost halted. Recipients of rent subsidies must now contribute a higher proportion of their income to their housing costs than previously. Most housing assistance is provided under long-term agreements which continue to be honored; therefore, the effects of these cuts will be felt more strongly as rental and mortgage subsidy agreements expire over the next decade. As these agreements expire, it is also likely that more low-income housing will be converted into units that only the more affluent can afford.

The shortage of adequate shelter for low-income households is critical, and contributes to the rising homeless population. A 1985 General Accounting Office study estimated that almost half of households with 50 percent or less of median family income paid more than half of their income for rent and one in five lived in inadequate units, lacking either plumbing, kitchen facilities, common areas, heating, or electricity.[6]

As a result of the retrenchments in the early 1980s, a smaller proportion of the working poor were lifted out of poverty by in-kind benefits in 1985 than in 1980. At the same time, and in part because of subsequent benefit restorations, the percentage of working poor receiving various in-kind benefits has remained essentially the same.

Social Insurance Programs

Federal social insurance programs help provide nonmeans-tested support for workers when they retire, lose their jobs, or become disabled. In contrast to means-tested programs which are financed out of general revenue, social insurance programs are financed by payroll taxes. The social insurance program outlays are triple the expenditures for means-tested programs. By virtue of their universal coverage, the social insurance programs enjoy widespread public support.

Social security is the largest and most acclaimed income support program. It is of particular help to retired low-wage workers. In 1986, some 33.5 million retired workers or their survivors received social security retirement benefits at a cost of $182 billion. The 1983 revision of social security was designed to ensure that the system remain financially sound for the balance of the twentieth century and beyond.

One in three of the elderly was impoverished in 1960. Primarily because of more generous social security benefits, that proportion fell to one in eight by 1985. In 1984 social security and railroad retirement benefits reduced poverty among the elderly by 74 percent. Almost 13 million individuals aged sixty-five and over were lifted above the poverty line by these benefits. Lenient employment and earnings requirements extend social security benefits to most low-wage workers, and benefit levels are weighted in favor of these workers.

Low-wage workers are dependent on social security benefits in their retirement years either because their employers do not frequently provide retirement benefits or because the high turnover rate associated with their jobs prevent them from acquiring private vesting rights for pensions. The poor who work part time are especially unlikely to receive pension benefits. In 1984 only one in four full-time year-round impoverished workers and 11 percent of all poor wage and salary workers were covered by pensions. The 1986 change in pension laws reduced the vesting requirement from ten years to five years. Whether this change will help an appreciable number of working poor to acquire vesting rights is unknown, but needless to say, low-wage workers not covered by a private pension are hardly in a position to save for the future.

The $20 billion disability insurance (DI) program provides income support to workers with severe disabilities that prevent gainful employment. The DI program expanded rapidly from its inception in 1956 until the late 1970s, coincident with the drop in labor force participation of adult male workers between the ages of fifty-five and sixty-four.

Labor force participation of males aged 55–64

1970	83.0%
1980	72.1
1985	67.4

The convergence of these trends led to the institution of more stringent review of applications to prevent program abuse. As a result, the number of disability insurance recipients fell from 2.9 million in 1979 to 2.7 million in 1985; the total number of beneficiaries, including spouses and children, fell from 4.8 million to 3.9 million. The increase in labor force withdrawal among elderly males is explained by rising standards of living, social security, pension benefits, medicare, and the use of the DI program. Disabled workers also receive assistance from the means-tested supplemental security income program and the sizable state workers' compensation programs. It is difficult to determine precisely what disabilities prevent employment, but further reductions in the DI rolls may lead to denying support to severely disabled individuals who cannot work.

The unemployment insurance (UI) system, funded by a tax on payrolls paid by employers, provides temporary income support to workers who involuntarily lose their jobs. The program has generally fulfilled its missions of providing a temporary income cushion for the unemployed and of acting as a countercyclical stimulus during recessions. The program tends to be of greatest benefit to blue-collar workers who are occasionally forced into temporary unemployment.

Unemployment insurance does prevent poverty for some of the unemployed, but, in general, low-wage workers are not well served by the UI system because of its low payroll tax base and because their unstable part-time employment may not meet UI work requirements. Tighter state administrative controls, the sharp retrenchment in federal additional benefit programs, an increase in the proportion of long-term unemployed, more women in the workplace (who are less likely to meet UI earnings and employment requirements), and the shift to service sector employment (which, if intermittent, may preclude UI eligibility) all have contributed to a reduction in the proportion of the unemployed who are eligible for UI benefits. In 1986, only one in three persons counted as unemployed received benefits—a historic low.

The federal maximum taxable UI wage base of $7,000 is less that one-sixth of the social security taxable base. A boost in the UI taxable base would provide revenues that could tilt benefits in favor of low-wage workers and expand protection to workers forced into unemployment.

How Much Assistance?

Means-tested cash assistance programs provide little aid to the working poor unless they are disabled (Table 9). AFDC, the largest federal cash assistance program, mostly helps female-headed families. Even in states in which unemployed two-parent families are eligible, few receive assistance.

Means-tested in-kind benefit programs are of more help to the working poor than cash assistance. The working and nonworking poor are equally eligible to receive food stamps, although a smaller percentage of the former take advantage of the program. Medicaid is targeted to the aged, disabled, and AFDC recipients but also benefits some families with low earnings. The public housing and rent supplement programs have no categorical restrictions that exclude the working poor, but their low funding level prevents them from serving most of potentially eligible recipients.

Although the disability and unemployment insurance programs were both reduced in the 1980s, the social insurance system remained relatively generous in the mid-1980s. These programs benefit individuals of all income levels and are of substantial assistance to the poor. The working poor do not receive much help while they are working but are treated more

Table 9. Welfare and social insurance programs provide limited help to the working poor

Program	1986 Outlays (in Billions)	Target Group	Assistance to Working Poor
Means-tested cash assistance			
AFDC	$ 15.9	Female-headed families	Minimal
AFDC-UP	1.8	Two-parent families with unemployment	None to moderate
Means-tested in-kind benefits			
Food stamps	$ 12.6	All low-income families	Moderate
Medicaid	44.7	Aged, disabled, and AFDC recipients	Minimal to moderate
Housing assistance	11.2	Households with incomes less than 50% of median income	Minimal
Social insurance			
Social security	$182.0	Elderly and dependents	Substantial
Disability insurance	20.2	Severely disabled	Moderate
Unemployment insurance	17.8	Involuntary job losers	Minimal to moderate

Source: Office of Management and Budget and House Ways and Means Committee

generously once they reach retirement age, become disabled, or involuntarily lose their jobs. Universal programs or efforts that benefit individuals who demonstrably cannot help themselves have greater public support than programs that target the working poor. The latter programs tend to be depicted inaccurately as unnecessary or as encouraging indolence among individuals who could lift themselves out of poverty.

State and federal governments spend substantial sums on preparation for work through the basic education system and aid to college education. Those who fail or are failed by this system are more likely to receive in-kind or income assistance that alleviates immediate need than to benefit from employment assistance that would help them escape poverty and lead to economic self-sufficiency. Expenditures on social insurance, in-kind benefits, and income-assistance programs dwarf outlays for second-chance employment and training programs. This is not an efficient use of government funds. In contrast to investment in training, most income-support program costs are not offset by productivity increases or declines in other areas of government spending. There are exceptions to this generalization. For example, the prevention of malnutrition among the children of the working poor by the food stamps program not only helps these children become productive citizens, but tends to reduce medical costs. Although promoting economic self-sufficiency is the best long-term approach to the problems of the working poor, if working fails to bring individuals and their families out of poverty, income-support programs provide necessary assistance to them.

Work Programs for Welfare Recipients

Most of the recent discussions of the welfare system have focused on the able-bodied poor who do not work. Tales of families with able-bodied adults "living off the dole" undermine support for all welfare programs as well as employment and training assistance. Clearly there are some impoverished adults who make little effort to help themselves, but the focus on these individuals obscures the problems of those who seek but cannot find jobs and those who work but do not earn sufficient wages to escape from poverty.

In the context of this discussion, it is important to examine welfare policies for the able-bodied but nonworking poor. Improving their prospects would reduce the high cost to society which results both from their antisocial behavior and from welfare expenditures.

The welfare policy debate has recently centered on requiring welfare recipients to work off the assistance they receive. This debate has been spurred by concern over welfare costs and by anecdotes of welfare freeloaders, as well as by the Reagan administration's opposition to most income support for the able-bodied poor. President Reagan consistently introduced and supported workfare proposals which, in their simplest form, required welfare recipients to work off their welfare grants.

Reagan administration efforts led to the passage of the 1981 legislation that gave states the option to establish mandatory or voluntary AFDC workfare programs. Although some of these welfare and work programs have shown some promise, it does not necessarily follow that mandatory workfare is a realistic option. Experimental state programs differ substantially from simple mandatory workfare. They more closely resemble employment and training programs which include temporary work in a public service job.

Approaches

The 1935 Social Security Act created the first permanent federally funded program in aid of destitute mothers and their children. In response to the then prevailing massive unemployment and society's belief that mothers of small children should not be required to work, the act was based on the assumption that work and welfare were mutually exclusive. In the 1960s Congress expanded the AFDC program to include, at the option of the states, two-parent households. By 1967, increased interest in helping the poor help themselves for both altruistic reasons and in the interest of reducing welfare expenditures led Congress to enact the Work Incentive (WIN) program.

WIN was intended to provide registrants with a variety of job-related services, including basic education, training, child care, and other support services; the law requires employable welfare parents with children over the age of six to register for work and training. Low funding levels have meant, however, that only a minority of AFDC recipients have been able to take advantage of WIN services. Moreover, the program has often focused on employable recipients who might well have found jobs on their own. On the other hand, a 1982 General Accounting Office study found that about half of WIN participants believed that program participation did help them find a job.[7] Although Congress repeatedly rejected Reagan administration proposals to abolish WIN, expenditures fell from $381 million in fiscal 1981 to an estimated $110 million in fiscal 1987.

The 1981 Omnibus Budget Reconciliation Act (OBRA) gives the states the option to require adult AFDC recipients to perform community work in exchange for their welfare grant. By mid-1986, twenty-three states, with varying degrees of participation, had adopted community work experience programs (CWEP). States have used the substantial latitude given them by OBRA to offer a wide range of work and welfare programs. The type of employment and training services offered, the scale of the initiatives, whether or not participation is mandatory or voluntary, and the group of targeted recipients all vary from state to state. Differences in program structure are reflective of substantial differences in program goals; for example, one state may emphasize education and skill training whereas another emphasizes immediate job placement.[8]

An ongoing comprehensive evaluation of work and welfare initiatives by the Manpower Development Research Corporation (MDRC) has found moderately encouraging results. Program participants experienced modest positive employment gains compared to nonparticipants. Though the required work experience demanded only a low level of skill, supervisors considered the work performed as useful and participants generally had positive reactions to both working and their particular work assignments. A study of work and welfare initiatives in Ohio found that those programs were popular among both administrators and participants.[9]

The state welfare and work programs are not simple workfare programs nor do they represent altogether new approaches. MDRC found that job-search assistance and unpaid work experiences of limited duration were the major options offered to participants. One of the most encouraging work and welfare programs, the Massachusetts Employment and Training (ET) program, includes no work requirement. Instead, voluntary enrollees can choose between a mix of education, training, and placement services. This high-cost program also provides child care services and reimbursement for transportation outlays.

Many current work and welfare programs differ little from

prior WIN programs; work experience assignments are often similar to job slots in past public service employment programs. What is new is the increased emphasis placed on work and welfare programs and the intense interest in assessing the effectiveness of the programs.[10] This interest has led to growing consensus on the need to design programs that move welfare recipients into gainful employment. Most states, however, have not been willing to contribute the significant up-front outlays necessary for a comprehensive program.

An Ongoing Experiment

In its 1988 budget, the Reagan administration proposed the Greater Opportunity and Welfare (GROW) program calling for phased-in mandatory participation quotas that would include 60 percent of all registered AFDC recipients by its fifth year. In addition, the food stamp program requires each state to implement an employment-related program for all recipients by April 1987. The vagueness of this legislation makes it difficult to predict the nature of the resulting programs.

At the state level, improvement of the employment prospects of welfare recipients through work requirements is a basic element of the new welfare reform programs. California's Greater Avenues for Independence (GAIN) program is a potentially important approach. GAIN, which was passed in 1985 with bipartisan support, offers a comprehensive range of job training and placement services combined with a community work requirement for participants if initial job placement efforts fail.

Work and welfare initiatives deserve expansion. Income support is essential but many AFDC recipients facing significant employment barriers require a comprehensive program if they are to find sustained employment. Temporary work experiences can give participants the opportunity to compete for jobs, enhance their dignity, and perform useful community services. Work requirements for welfare recipients are supported by a vast majority of the public.[11] If it were clear that government assistance is targeted primarily to those who cannot help themselves, or who do work but cannot raise themselves out of poverty, or who work in return for benefits, public support for more generous antipoverty programs might increase.

This observation is not intended to suggest that mandatory workfare can effectively be implemented on a national basis. A number of important issues must first be resolved. Who should work requirements apply to? How can jobs be created without displacing public employees? How can sanctions be effectively applied without harming children of uncooperative parents? What pay level should recipients receive? Is it fair to pay them less than permanent employees make on the same job?

It is also not clear that work requirements are better than public service jobs programs. In both cases, a needy individual temporarily works for the government or a nonprofit institution in return for wages. Many workfare jobs, in fact, closely resemble the public service employment jobs criticized by the Reagan administration. Public service employment programs, however, can serve—within budget constraints—other needy individuals (not just AFDC recipients). In addition, participation in the program involves a paycheck as well as the satisfaction of working on a productive job as opposed to just working off a welfare check.

Work requirements have a positive or negative impact depending on their design and on how they fit into comprehensive employment and training programs for welfare recipients. An effective program must include individual needs assessments, skill training, job search help, production work slots, and competent administrative staff. Imposing a work requirement is not in itself an effective policy; welfare and work programs must also include comprehensive assessment, training, and placement programs.

Current work and welfare initiatives provide, at best, only a partial solution to the poverty problem. Policy makers and the public need to recognize that these programs can only moderately reduce welfare costs. To increase productivity of low-skilled individuals requires comprehensive programs with significant upfront investments. The scope of current efforts remains limited. Workfare programs neglect the needs of impoverished individuals who already have jobs as well as the employability problems of impoverished adult males who do not receive welfare. Females who head households may be able to work, but it may be neither feasible nor socially desirable for them to work full time. In order to raise such women out of poverty, work and welfare must go together. In addition, the effectiveness of programs designed to improve skills and those which ease the transition from welfare to private employment depends on the state of the economy and the availability of jobs. One reason for the claimed success of Massachusetts' ET program is that state's booming economy. In a less prosperous state, this program model might be helpful, but would not achieve as high a placement rate.

Nevertheless, existing welfare to work experiments are encouraging and contain elements beneficial both to participants and the public. States should continue to have the latitude to experiment with and augment program approaches. Effective projects will vary from state to state or even from locality to locality, depending on the characteristics of the welfare population, the experience and quality of administrators, and the health of the area's economy.

Work Incentives and Welfare Reform

The complexity of the welfare and social insurance system makes it difficult to isolate its effect on work incentives. The lack of solid data has not, however, prevented heated discussion and strong opinions about the impact of the welfare system on the incentive to work.

The concern with the work incentive elements of the welfare system is justified. Those who do work do not want to contribute tax dollars to those who are able to work but make no effort to do so. The welfare system should be designed to assist those who cannot work, those who are unsuccessfully looking for work, and those who work and remain in poverty. All of these groups find it difficult to obtain acceptable levels of income and should be deemed "deserving" of public support.

The administration's call for mandatory workfare for AFDC recipients is not viable without the funding necessary to implement such programs effectively. Existing state employment and training programs for welfare recipients that promote economic self-sufficiency should be explored and encouraged. The workfare discussion focuses, however, on the idle poor and ignores the pressing needs of the working poor and the failure of the welfare system to address their problems.

The welfare system does provide a measure of economic security to individuals of all income levels but it falls short in helping the working poor and their families to meet their basic needs. The debate over work disincentives should not blind policy makers to the necessity of efforts to assist the working poor. Inadequate assistance to those working but poor is a powerful work disincentive and a cause of deprivation.

8. Looking Down the Road

The mid-1980s were kinder to the working poor than the first part of the decade. The 1981 cuts in programs that provide assistance to the working poor gave way either to program stability or to moderate restorations, and the 1986 tax reform law extended substantial relief to low-income families.

Four years of economic recovery, however, put only a slight dent into the number of working poor, and the unemployment rate remained in the 7 percent range, a recession level by historic standards. Other developments offer little hope for tighter labor markets for the balance of the decade: international competition continues to contribute to the disappearance of jobs, pockets of economic dislocation abound, millions of adults lack basic skills, and a recession looms on the horizon. The partial restoration that has occurred to the programs designed to offer aid to the working poor will lift few of them out of poverty.

Unabashed advocates of free market economies argue that the best labor policy is to let the market work its course and that government intervention, particularly at the federal level, exacerbates labor market problems. Accordingly, the Reagan administration opposes increasing job-training funding and rejects job creation as a tool for assisting the unemployed. The administration also generally opposes welfare assistance as a last resort for the working poor, arguing that able-bodied adults can take care of themselves and that extending support will only encourage indolence. The administration's policies seem to focus on getting the poor off welfare without regard to whether they escape poverty.

Liberals reject this purely market-oriented approach and favor a reaffirmation of a positive role for government and modifications of the policies that dominated the American scene throughout the 1980s. To ease the problems of the working poor, they advocate reducing unemployment through expansionary macroeconomic policy, increasing the minimum wage, expanding employment and training programs, and supplementing earnings of poor workers with means-tested assistance programs.

The current political climate and the large budget deficit make efforts to increase assistance to the working poor difficult. In the not too distant future, however, the problems of poverty and the working poor are bound to reemerge on the nation's agenda. Delay in addressing these problems will increase the direct and indirect burden on future generations.

The Need for Federal Intervention

Sustained economic growth helps the working poor but is only a partial remedy. In the middle of the fifth year of recovery from the 1981–82 recession, over 6 percent of all Americans who sought work could not find jobs and the number of working poor fell only slightly from the recessionary high.

The low economic growth rate had only a marginal effect on reducing the number of working poor. Even if the pace of growth is accelerated, in the absence of increased federal intervention the convergence of work and poverty will continue to mar the lives of millions of individuals and their families. Sustained economic growth would benefit the working poor in some areas, but rural and ghetto economies can remain weak even if the nearby areas prosper. The mismatch between available jobs and the skill levels of the unemployed or underemployed also need to be addressed. The millions of Americans who lack basic skills will not find higher-paying jobs even in an expanding national economy.

In 1986 over 8 million Americans remained unemployed, 5.6 million workers were employed part time because they could not find full-time work, and 1.1 million individuals became discouraged and gave up looking for jobs. Deep recession conditions continued to prevail in several states, from Alaska to Texas. Even in states with below average unemployment rates, there were metropolitan areas with seriously troubled economies. In California, double-digit unemployment rates persisted in Bakersfield, Fresno, Modesto, and Stockton. In Indiana, the Gary-Hammond area, home of many abandoned steel mills, had 10.8 percent unemployment. In the nation's capital, the metropolitan area had a 3.4 percent unemployment rate but poverty-stricken areas were common within the city. A reduction in the national unemployment rate will help but will not come close to solving these localized labor market problems.

Ongoing economic trends do not bode well for the working poor. In addition to the high unemployment rate, income distribution is becoming more skewed in favor of the affluent. Record high trade deficits continue to contribute to loose labor markets, causing a loss of jobs and dampening wage growth.

The net effect of demographic trends on the working poor is uncertain. The number of youth entering the work force fell sharply throughout the 1980s and this trend will continue into the 1990s. The dwindling supply of young workers should improve their employment and earnings prospects. However, the current minority youth unemployment rate of around 40 percent shows little prospect of abating.

The rate of new women entrants into the workplace will also affect the low-wage labor market. Changes in this rate reflect a complex web of socioeconomic factors and are hard to predict, but the expected continued entrance of women into the labor force will both directly and indirectly add to the supply of low-wage workers and act as a wage depressant. Female-headed households also have a high probability of remaining poor even while working.

Many questions are yet to be answered about the absorption of immigrants into the labor force and the effects of the 1986 immigration law. It is unlikely, however, that the act will cut off immigration; the United States remains a land of safety and opportunity. New immigrants will continue to compete with the working poor for jobs in low wage labor markets. Uncertainty surrounds estimates for the number of immigrants and changes in labor force participation by women, but the net change in labor supply is expected to be positive.

Following the decline in inflation, federal macroeconomic policy in the mid-1980s tilted toward promoting economic growth. Interest rates dropped, providing a monetary stimulus to the economy. The large federal deficit provided a substantial fiscal stimulus. Other federal policies extended direct relief to the working poor. The 1986 tax law included provisions of tremendous benefit to this group. After sharp cuts in the early 1980s, employment and training funding was stabilized. Some earlier policy changes in the means-tested assistance programs were partially restored by Congress.

With the significant exception of tax reform, these policy changes, though helpful, were limited in scope. The Reagan administration, with a strong assist by the Federal Reserve Bank, opposed an active federal government role to reduce the unemployment rate further. Tough talk about trade by politicians from both parties has not led to declining trade deficits. The purchasing power of the minimum wage remains at its lowest level in over thirty years, sharply limiting the opportunities for low-wage workers without other sources of income to earn their way out of poverty. Programs that promote economic self-sufficiency are funded at a minuscule level relative to the barriers the unskilled face in finding gainful employment. Welfare programs for the working poor require further restoration after the cuts of the early 1980s. Current policies are likely to lead to continued high levels of poverty among individuals and families who are making considerable work efforts.

A Positive and Affordable Agenda

In some areas, the optimum policy agenda to aid the working poor would not differ dramatically from current policies. Macroeconomic policy obviously must be designed with many objectives in mind; the working poor is only one segment of society that would benefit from tight labor markets. With the federal deficit already disturbingly high, an even more expansionary fiscal policy is an inappropriate approach to stimulating economic demand.

Both trade and immigration policies should strike the right balance between complex and sometimes conflicting objectives. Trade policy should focus on obtaining access for American exports to foreign markets, weighing the costs of protectionism to the domestic and international economies against the need to limit the loss of jobs from rising imports. Immigration policy should balance the objectives of offering opportunities and a haven to the economically or politically oppressed of all nations with the objectives of tight labor markets and raising working standards.

In other policy areas, however, a significant departure from the course of current policies is necessary to implement an affordable agenda to help the working poor. Rather than equating most of the able-bodied poor with those not requiring assistance, the alternative agenda is based on the belief that the working poor do require assistance. Some of the poor could be doing more to lift themselves out of poverty, but the government should not only facilitate this path, it should also assist those who are already working. This policy agenda reflects the belief that government can and should help create jobs, raise wages, break down employment barriers, provide skill training, and, when necessary, contribute to the income security of the working poor.

Some of the policy changes necessary to adopt this agenda would not increase government expenditures. The statutory federal minimum wage can ensure that working full time year round provides the opportunity to escape poverty. It can also help combat the feminization of poverty, as women are disproportionately affected by the minimum wage. The minimum wage should be raised to 50 percent of the average private nonsupervisory nonagricultural wage, a level equivalent to the goal that has been intermittently achieved since the end of World War II. As of early 1987, the minimum wage of $3.35 per hour was at its lowest inflation-adjusted level in thirty-two years; it fell well short of providing income sufficient for even a family of three to escape poverty. The minimum wage should be raised gradually to facilitate smooth market adjustments. The proposed increase, to be achieved over several years, would amount to a little over a $1 increase per hour in 1987 dollars. Indexing the minimum wage at 50 percent of the average wage would ensure that minimum-wage workers continue to share in the benefits of economic growth. Raising the minimum wage is a good approach, but not a costless one. Business costs would be raised and some employment loss would occur.

Congress, in addition, should enact legislation raising the penalties for willful violations of the minimum-wage statute, and vigorous enforcement is essential if low-wage workers are to be protected. Exemptions from the Fair Labor Standards Act should be carefully reviewed because some of these are no longer justified; in particular, retail trade and service establishment exemptions should be limited.

The federal government should also enforce equal employment opportunity laws more effectively and take the lead in reaffirming the nation's commitment to a society without discrimination. To accelerate the advancement of minorities and women in the workplace, the EEOC should reduce its case backlog, pursue affirmative action, and emphasize class-based relief, a strategy that would reap many benefits but would have minimal impact on federal outlays.

Other needed policy modifications would increase federal expenditures. Larger outlays alone will not solve the problems of the working poor, but some increases are necessary. Programs to promote economic self-sufficiency through skill training and easing of labor market adjustments can be expensive in the short run; by increasing employment they can, however, achieve some savings in the long term through lower welfare expenditure and greater government revenue. A precise estimate of these savings is impossible; they will be significant but may not completely offset initial outlays. Though means-tested programs, with some significant exceptions, are not offset by other savings, they provide essential income and service support.

The overall cost of programs for the working poor must be considered against the substantial resources devoted to income security programs for the general population. Government assistance is distributed to all income classes. The proposed changes should be funded by selected changes in the tax code.

The proposals discussed here would require raising outlays by about $10 billion annually. If alleviating the difficulties faced by the working poor is accepted as a national priority, this level of increase is reasonable. The increases should be spread over several years, both because of the high federal deficit and because programs such as job training must be expanded slowly if they are to be optimally effective (Table 10).

Estimating the amount of federal dollars currently spent to assist the working poor is a complicated task. Some programs do

Table 10. Federal increases necessary to help the working poor escape poverty

Program	Total	Estimated share for working poor (in millions, 1986 outlays)	Recommended increase
Earned income tax credit	$ 2,115	$ 1,600	$ 0
Adult education	104	80	200
Vocational education	931	310	0
JTPA, II-A	1,911	1,700	1,900
Job Corps	594	550	200
Vocational rehabilitation	1,145	700	0
Social Servies Block Grant	2,671	900	600
Head Start	1,051	350	200
Employment service	769	250	100
Targeted Jobs Tax Credit	510	460	0
Public service employment	0	0	2,500
Summer youth employment	746	670	0
Employment of older Americans	321	290	0
AFDC and AFDC-UP	17,700	1,100	1,700
AFDC changes, secondary effects	0	0	600
Food stamps	12,600	3,200	0
Medicaid	44,725	1,600	0
Federally subsidized health insurance	0	0	700
Housing assistance	11,222	2,150	1,100
Work incentive program	227	200	200
Total	99,342	16,110	10,000

Sources: Office of Management and Budget and assorted government departments.

Note: Programs are listed in the order they are discussed in this study. Outlays consist of federal expenditures except for AFDC (47% state expenditures), food stamps (8% state expenditures), and medicaid (44% state expenditures). Table includes earned income and targeted jobs tax credits which are tax expenditures not outlays. Estimated share for working poor are authors' rough estimates intended to indicate ballpark amounts.

not provide income and employment data for recipients and some programs defy easy categorization. For example, skill training almost exclusively assists idle individuals, some of whom may not be actively seeking work. However, training prepares the poor for meaningful employment and is thus considered as assistance to the working poor.

The recommended sharp increases in several of the programs are justified either because expenditures have always been too low or because the recommended increase would restore the programs to their 1981 funding levels. Even with large increases, many individuals in the populations targeted by various programs will not be served. Education and training programs would receive the largest increase relative to their current size, but all basic assistance areas would be expanded (Figures 11 and 12).

A top priority should be the expansion of second-chance education and training programs. Without basic skills, workers are

Figure 11. Increased education, training, and employment outlays should be the highest priority.

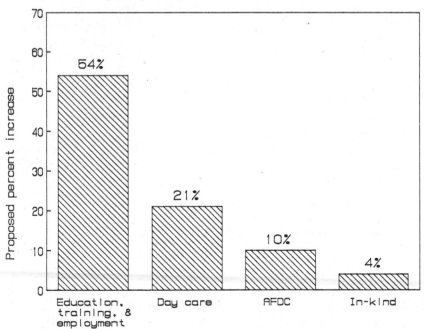

Figure 12. Proposed increases in aid of the working poor should be distributed across all program areas.

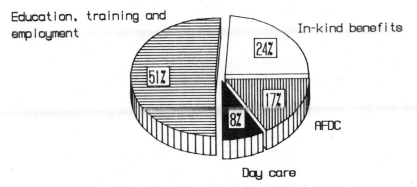

Education, training and employment

In-kind benefits

51%

24%

17%

8%

AFDC

Day care

destined to have jobs with low earnings or no jobs at all. Opportunities for basic skill training should be increased for those whose employment prospects are bleak either through the Job Corps or adult basic education or training programs. Raising Job Corps outlays by one-third would cost $200 million and tripling federal commitment to the adult basic education program would carry a price tag of about $200 million. The problems of the estimated 17 to 21 million illiterate adults and 4 million high school dropouts aged sixteen to twenty-four years require federal intervention if they are to be addressed. Doubling the size of the basic JTPA program, at a cost of $1.9 billion, would help the unemployed acquire jobs and enhance the opportunities of the working poor to improve their skills. The increased JTPA funding is needed to expand job search assistance and the scope and duration of training, including the payment of stipends on a selective basis.

Greater federal financing of day care will not only increase the level of employment among impoverished parents, but will improve child care for the young. A $600 million increase in the social services block grant would partially restore the cuts made in this program since 1981 and should be allocated solely to day care for the children of the working poor. Funding of the successful Head Start program has not been cut in recent years, but a 20 percent increase in the program (at a cost of $200 million) would enable it to reach a higher proportion of the targeted population.

Increasing the funding of the employment service by $100 million would improve its ability to generate job listings and develop better data processing systems. The Targeted Jobs Tax Credit program could be improved without higher government expenditures. The cost of strengthening administrative oversight would be offset by the savings generated by decreased employer use of the credit for already hired employees. If the credit is applied to higher-wage levels and used only for long-term jobs, the quality of TJTC placements will improve.

Public service jobs are a necessary component in assisting able-bodied adults who cannot find jobs. The number of unemployed far exceeds the number of job vacancies. When job search and skill training fail to result in gainful employment, unemployed adults should be able to obtain public service jobs paying at least the minimum wage. The size of the public service employment program should vary with economic conditions. A $2.5 billion program would provide about 250,000 job slots annually.

Means-tested assistance to the working poor needs to be strengthened. The earnings disregard should be returned to pre-OBRA status, at a cost to federal and state governments of about $600 million. The AFDC-UP program should be made mandatory, enabling two-parent families in all the states, instead of just half the states, to receive AFDC payments. The elimination of the ninety-nine-hour-per-month work limit for two-parent families would allow full-time workers at low wages to be eligible for income supplements. If benefits to new recipients are limited to six months, the proposed AFDC-UP changes would require added AFDC outlays of about $1.1 billion with a more adequate welfare system for two-parent families encouraging a more stable family structure. Even though the proposed changes will help the working poor meet their basic needs, most will still remain in poverty after receiving the transfers because of the low level of AFDC benefits.

Changes in the AFDC program have ripple effects on other programs. As AFDC income rises, outlays for food stamps and general assistance fall. However, those newly eligible for AFDC automatically qualify for medicaid. The annual increase in medicaid benefits would exceed the drop in other benefits by an estimated $600 million.[1]

A health insurance program for low-wage workers is an alternative to medicaid. The program would require $700 million in subsidies to finance a moderately sized effort. Increasing housing assistance by one-tenth at a cost of $1.1 billion would alleviate the critical lack of low-cost housing. One-quarter of this increase should be targeted to the homeless. Some of the public service jobs slots should be used for the repair or renovation of low-income housing.

The final recommendation would increase funding of the WIN program by $200 million. The added resources could help a greater number of welfare recipients move into productive employment. The current public desire to move welfare recipients into economic self-sufficiency has not been matched by program expenditures. On the contrary, Congress cut the 1987 WIN appropriations by half.

There are many options for raising federal revenues in a progressive and fair manner that would more than make up for the recommended added expenditures. One alternative is to raise the top federal income tax bracket for the affluent to 33 percent, still less than half the 1981 rate of 70 percent, which would generate about $6.5 billion in revenue in 1989. Tax expenditures that primarily aid high-income families could be further restricted. For example if tax savings from the mortgage interest deduction were limited to 15 percent of interest paid (equal to the value of the lowest tax bracket) about $9.5 billion would be raised in 1989. Another option is to tax 50 percent of all social security benefits (instead of the current procedure of only taxing 50 percent of benefits over an income threshold), and this option would raise revenues of about $7.1 billion in 1989.[2]

The increased costs necessary to assist the working poor should also be weighed against the costs of inaction. In the past few years, the federal government has reduced its role in promoting tight labor markets and assisting the working poor. The costs have been higher unemployment, more poverty, added deprivation, and greater dependency on government.

Which Path Will Be Followed?

Although there is renewed interest in welfare reform in early 1987, measures to help the working poor will probably face heavy sledding. The 100th Congress may vote to raise the minimum wage and increase funding for training and welfare programs, but President Reagan may veto such measures. Free market ideology has strong political support and mitigates against the adoption of stronger federal worker protections, and the large federal budget deficit militates against the expansion of almost all programs. Politicians who favor reducing tax expenditures for the middle class or raising the top tax rate are scarce. Most of all, in 1987 the Reagan administration remained adamantly opposed to a strong federal government role in assisting the poor.

Support for federal intervention tends to be cyclical. Retrenchments in the 1980s reflected, in part, disgruntlement with the less than dramatic effects of stepped-up federal efforts to combat poverty. Indeed, the problems of the poor are frequently intractable, but many government programs have been more successful than is generally known or believed. The Job Corps has assisted disadvantaged teenagers who are likely to remain among the hard-core unemployed. Cash assistance has alleviated deprivation and food stamps and medicaid have improved diets and health care. If these successes are made known, and the problems of the poor continue, political pressure might shift in favor of stronger federal programs. In fact, recent polls indicate that, although the public remains skeptical about the effectiveness of government efforts, the majority of the population supports increased spending on poverty programs, especially in the areas of education and training and job creation.[3] Notwithstanding the changes of recent years, the structure of antipoverty programs remains intact. A new system does not need to be constructed, the old system needs to be repaired.

The working poor as a group is well positioned to benefit from renewed public support of affirmative government action. They do try to help themselves but, in their struggle for economic self-sufficiency, they are often defeated. The millions of working poor confound the long-ingrained belief and hope prevalent in this nation that work leads to an adequate if not prosperous life. Their existence undermines the truism that a commitment to the work ethic provides a road out of poverty.

Targeted federal government policies are only one component of a commitment aimed at reducing the persistence of work with poverty. State and local governments, the private sector, other institutions, and, of course, impoverished individuals themselves must all act together if the ranks of the working poor are to diminish. At the same time, a positive and active role for the federal government is a crucial element in adequately addressing the difficulties of this nation's needy citizens. That element should be restored.

Notes

2. Profile of the Working Poor

1. Richard S. Belous, Linda H. LeGrande, Brian W. Caskill, "Middle-Class Erosion and Growing Income Inequality: Fact or Fiction," Congressional Research Service, November 28, 1985, pp. 27, 30.

2. U.S. Department of Education, "Update on Adult Illiteracy," April 14, 1986 (processed).

3. U.S. Bureau of the Census, *Labor Force Status and Other Characteristics of Persons with a Work Disability: 1982* (Washington, D.C.: U.S. Government Printing Office, July 1983), Series P-23, no. 127, pp. 33, 35.

4. David T. Ellwood, "Divide and Conquer: Responsible Security for America's Poor Families," Ford Foundation Project on the Future of the Social Welfare State, November 1986, p. 12.

5. Katherine G. Abraham, "Structural/Frictional vs. Deficient Demand Unemployment: Some New Evidence," *American Economic Review,* September 1983, p. 722.

6. U.S. Bureau of the Census, *Estimates of Poverty including the Value of Noncash Benefits: 1985,* Technical Paper 56, p. 7.

7. Martha S. Hill, "Some Dynamic Aspects of Poverty," in *Five Thousand American Families—Patterns of Economic Progress, vol. 9, Analyses of the First Twelve Years of the Panel Study of Income Dynamics,* ed. Martha S. Hill, Daniel H. Hill, and James N. Morgan (Ann Arbor, Mich.: Institute for Social Research, University of Michigan, 1981), pp. 102, 112; Greg J. Duncan, *Years of Poverty, Years of Plenty* (Ann Arbor, Mich.: Institute for Social Research, University of Michigan, 1984), p. 41.

8. Mary Jo Bane and David T. Ellwood, "Slipping into and out of Poverty: The Dynamics of Spells," *Journal of Human Resources,* Winter 1986, pp. 1–7.

9. Ibid., p. 19.

10. Hill, p. 112; Duncan, pp. 61–65 (both cited in no. 7, above).

11. Charles Murray (with Deborah Laren), "According to Age: Longitudinal Profile of AFDC recipients and the Poor by Age Group," prepared for the Marquette University and American Enterprise Institute Working Seminar on the Family and American Welfare Policy, September 1986, p. 81.

12. Richard B. Freeman, "Troubled Workers in the Labor Market," *Seventh Annual Report: The Federal Interest in Employment and Training,* Appendix A (Washington, D.C.: National Commission for Employment Policy, October 1981), pp. 106, 112, 115.

3. Low-Wage Job Markets

1. Unpublished data supplied by the Income and Well-being Section of Economic Research Service, U.S. Department of Agriculture. These data will appear in a forthcoming publication of Peggy J. Ross and Elizabeth S. Morrissey.

2. U.S. Bureau of Labor Statistics, *Linking Employment Problems to Economic Status* (Washington, D.C.: Government Printing Office, Bureau of Labor Statistics Bulletin 2270, 1986).

3. National Commission on Employment and Unemployment Statistics, *Counting the Labor Force* (Washington, D.C.: Government Printing Office, 1979), chap. 5; Robert Taggart, *Hardship: The Welfare Consequences of Labor Market Problems* (Kalamazoo, Mich.: W. É. Upjohn Institute for Employment Research, 1982), chap. 1.

4. Thomas J. Lueck, "Rich and Poor: Widening Gap Seen for Area," *New York Times,* May 2, 1986, p. B1.

5. Neal H. Rosenthal, "The Shrinking Middle Class: Myth or Reality?" *Monthly Labor Review,* March 1985, pp. 7–8; Patrick J. McMahon and John H. Tschetter, "The Declining Middle Class: A Further Analysis," *Monthly Labor Review,* September 1986, p. 23.

6. U.S. Congress, Office of Technology Assessment, *Technology and Structural Unemployment: Reemploying Displaced Adults,* February 1986, pp. 376, 382, 392.

7. Valerie A. Personick, "A Second Look at Industry Output and Employment Trends through 1985," *Monthly Labor Review,* November 1985, p. 26.

8. "BLS Survey Shows Higher Rate of Reemployment Among Displaced Workers," *Employee Relations Weekly,* October 20, 1986, p. 1299.

9. Barry Bluestone and Bennett Harrison, "The Great American Job Machine: The Proliferation of Low-Wage Employment in the U.S. Economy," U.S. Congress, Joint Economic Committee, December 1986, p. 17.

10. Howard N. Fullerton, Jr., "The 1985 Labor Force: BLS' Latest Projections," *Monthly Labor Review,* November 1985, p. 20.

11. Ellen Sehgal, "Foreign Born in the U.S. Labor Market: The Results of a Special Survey," *Monthly Labor Review,* July 1985, p. 18.

12. Michael J. Piore, *Birds of Passage* (Cambridge: Cambridge University Press, 1979), p. 3.

13. Vernon M. Briggs, Jr., "Employment Trends and Contemporary Labor Policy," in *Immigration: Issues and policies,* ed. Vernon M. Briggs, Jr., and Marta Tienda (Washington, D.C.: National Council on Employment Policy, 1984), p. 17.

4. Making Work Pay

1. Earl F. Mellor and Steven E. Haugen, "Hourly Paid Workers: Who They are and What They Earn," *Monthly Labor Review,* February 1986, p. 25.

2. *Report of the Minimum Wage Study Commission,* vol. 1 (Washington, D.C.: U.S. Government Printing Office, 1981), pp. 19–21.

3. Congressional Budget Office, *The Minimum Wage: Its Relationship to Incomes and Poverty,* Staff Working Paper, June 1986, pp. 16–18.

4. *Study Commission,* p. 121.

5. Ibid., pp. 156, 158.

6. Statement of Congressman George Miller, *The Reemergence of Sweatshops and the Enforcement of Wage and Hour Standards of the Committee on Education and Labor,* U.S. House of Representatives, Subcommittee on Labor Standards of the Committee on Education and Labor, 1982, p. 4.

7. Edward M. Gramlich, "Impact of Minimum Wage on Other Wages, Employment, and Family Incomes," *Brookings Papers on Economic Activity,* 1976:2, pp. 419–52.

8. *Study Commission,* p. 38.

9. Gary Solon, "The Minimum Wage and Teenage Employment: A Reanalysis with Attention to Serial Correlation and Seasonality," *Journal of Human Resources,* Spring 1985, pp. 292–97.

10. Martha Brannigan, "A Shortage of Youths Brings Wide Changes to the Labor Market," *Wall Street Journal,* September 3, 1986, p. 11.

11. *Study Commission,* p. 47.

12. Rebecca M. Blank and Alan S. Blinder, "Macroeconomics, Income Distribution, and Poverty," in *Fighting Poverty: What Works and What Doesn't,* ed. Sheldon H. Danziger and Daniel H. Weinberg (Cambridge, Mass.: Harvard University Press, 1986), p. 198.

13. U.S. Congress, House Committee on Ways and Means, *Background Material and Data on Programs within the Jurisdiction of the Committee on Ways and Means,* March 3, 1986, p. 565.

14. U.S. Congress, Staff of the Joint Committee on Taxation, "Data on Distribution by Income Class of Effects of the Tax Reform Act of 1986," JCX-28-86, October 1, 1986, Tables 1 and 8.

15. Sheldon Danziger and Peter Gottschalk, Testimony, *Work and Poverty: The Special Problems of the Working Poor,* Hearing, U.S. Congress, Committee on Government Operations, December 12, 1985, p. 22; Center

on Budget and Policy Priorities, "Taxes on Working Poor Rise for Sixth Straight Year," Washington, D.C., April 9, 1986, p. 1.

16. Center on Budget and Policy Priorities, "Conference Agreement on Tax Reform of Major Benefit to Working Poor," Washington, D.C., September 18, 1986, pp. 1–3.

17. Robert D. Reischauer, "Welfare Reform and the Working Poor," in *Reducing Poverty and Dependence* (Washington, D.C.: Center for National Policy, 1987).

5. Removing Employment Obstacles

1. United States General Accounting Office, *School Dropouts: The Extent and Nature of the Problem,* GAO/HRD-86-106 BR (Gaithersburg, Md.: U.S. General Accounting Office, June 1986), pp. 2, 5, 6, 10.

2. Andrew Sum, Paul Harrington, and William Goedicke, "Basic Skills, High School Diplomas, and the Labor Force, Employment, Unemployment, and Earnings Experience in the United States," Center for Labor Market Studies, Northeastern University, report prepared for the Ford Foundation, May 1986, pp. 6, 8.

3. Gordon Berlin, Andrew Sum, and Robert Taggart, "Cutting Through," paper presented to the Ford Foundation Welfare State Committee, December 1986, pp. 12–14.

4. U.S. Department of Education, English Language Proficiency Survey, Adult Performance and Adult Composition Tables, December 1985.

5. Lindsey Gruson, "Widespread Illiteracy Burdens the Nation," *New York Times,* July 22, 1986, pp. C1–2.

6. U.S. Bureau of the Census, *Labor Force Status and Other Characteristics of Persons with a Work Disability: 1982,* Series P-23, July 1983, no. 127, pp. 33, 35.

7. U.S. Congress, Office of Technology Assessment, *Technology and Structural Unemployment: Reemploying Displaced Adults,* OTA-ITE-250, February 1986, p. 376.

8. Congressional Research Service, Education and Public Welfare Division, Information on Selected Federal Employment and Training Programs, June 5, 1985, pp. 34–35.

9. Gordon Berlin and Joanne Duhl, "Education, Equity, and Economic Excellence: The Critical Role of Second-Chance Basic Skills and Job Training Programs," Ford Foundation, August 30, 1984, p. 40.

10. Burt Barnow, *The Education Training and Work Experience of the Adult Labor Force from 1984 to 1995,* (Washington, D.C.: National Commission on Employment Policy, June 1985), p. 72.

11. Westat, Inc., *Transition Year Implementation of the Job Training Partnership Act,* January 1985, chap. 5, pp. 20–23; Grinker Associates, Inc., *An Independent Sector Assessment of the Job Training Partnership Act* (New York: Grinker Associates, July 1986), pp. vi–vii; Gary Orfield and Helene Slessarev, *Job Training under the New Federalism* (Chicago:

Illinois Unemployment and Job Training Research Project, 1986), pp. 191–92.

12. Office of Technology Assessment, *Technology and Structural Unemployment,* pp. 3–4.

13. Committee on Youth Employment Programs, *Youth Employment and Training Programs: The YEDPA Years,* ed. Charles L. Betsey, Robinson G. Hollister, Jr., and Mary R. Papageorgia (Washington, D.C.: National Academy Press, 1985), pp. 9, 111–14.

14. Richard V. Burkhauser and Robert H. Haveman, *Disability and Work: The Economics of American Policy* (Baltimore: Johns Hopkins University Press, 1982), pp. 68–69.

15. Robert Taggart, "A Review of CETA Training," in *The T in CETA,* ed. Sar A. Levitan and Garth L. Mangum (Kalamazoo, Mich.: W. E. Upjohn Institute for Employment Research, 1981), p. 111.

16. U.S. Department of Labor, Office of Federal Contract Compliance Programs, *Employment Patterns of Minorities and Women in Federal Contractor and Noncontractor Establishments* (Washington, D.C.: Government Printing Office, 1984).

17. *Wygant v. Jackson Board of Education,* U.S., 106 S.Ct. 1842 (1986); *Local 93 International Association of Firefighters v. City of Cleveland,* U.S., 106 S.Ct. 3063 (1986); *Local 28 of the Sheet Metal Workers' International Association v. Equal Employment Opportunity Commission,* U.S., 106 S.Ct. 3019 (1986).

18. *A Children's Defense Budget* (Washington, D.C.: Children's Defense Fund, 1986), p. 290.

19. David P. Weikart, "The Cost Effectiveness of High Quality Early Childhood Programs," U.S. Congress, House Select Committee on Children, Youth, and Families, June 30, 1983.

20. Sharon Stephan, "Child Day Care: The Scope of Federal Involvement," *CRS Review,* Library of Congress, September 1985.

6. Finding and Creating Jobs

1. U.S. General Accounting Office, *Information on the U.S. Employment Service's Programs, Activities, and Functions* (Washington, D.C.: General Accounting Office, April 30, 1982), p. 4.

2. Ibid., Appendix 1, p. 16.

3. SRI International, *A National Evaluation of the Impact of the United States Employment Service, Final Report,* prepared for U.S. Department of Labor, Employment and Training Administration, June 1983.

4. U.S. General Accounting Office, *Employment Service: More Job-seekers Should be Referred to Private Employment Agencies* (Washington, D.C.: General Accounting Office, March 1986), p. 3.

5. Sar A. Levitan and Frank Gallo, "The Targeted Jobs Tax Credit: An Uncertain and Unfinished Experiment," Center for Social Policy Studies, George Washington University, Washington, D.C., July 22, 1986.

6. John Bishop, ed., *Targeted Jobs Tax Credit: Findings from Employer Surveys* (Columbus, Ohio: Ohio State University, National Center for Research in Vocational Education, May 1985), pp. 24–25, 30–31.

7. Gary Burtless, "Are Targeted Wage Subsidies Harmful? Evidence from a Wage Voucher Experiment," *Industrial and Labor Relations Review,* October 1985, pp. 105–14; Wisconsin Department of Health and Social Services and Wisconsin University's Institute for Research on Poverty, "Jobs Tax Credits—The Report of the Wage Bill Subsidy Research Project, Phase 2," January 1982.

8. Bishop, ed., *Targeted Jobs Tax Credit,* p. 63.

9. Sandra Christensen, "The Targeted Jobs Tax Credit," Congressional Budget Office, in U.S. Congress, House Committee on Ways and Means, Subcommittee on Select Revenue Measures, *Targeted Jobs Tax Credit Extension,* April 10, 1984, pp. 58–59.

10. Macro Systems, Inc., *Final Process Analysis Report on the Implementation and Use of the Targeted Jobs Tax Credit (TJTC) Program,* U.S. Department of Labor, Employment and Training Administration, May 7, 1985, chap. 7, p. 1.

11. John Bishop, Ohio State University, National Center for Research in Vocational Education, phone conversation, March 14, 1986.

12. Edward C. Lorenz, Maryland TJTC coordinator, phone conversation, May 2, 1986.

13. Donald S. Howard, *The WPA and Federal Relief Policy* (New York: Russell Sage Foundation, 1943), pp. 19–35.

14. Robert F. Cook, Charles F. Adams, Jr., V. Lane Rawlins, and Associates, *Public Service Employment: The Experience of a Decade* (Kalamazoo, Mich.: W. E. Upjohn Institute for Employment Research, 1985), p. ix.

15. Clifford Johnson, *Direct Federal Job Creation: Key Issues,* U.S. House of Representatives, Committee on Education and Labor, October 1985, pp. 1–6.

16. Cook et al., *Public Service Employment,* pp. 50, 59, 128.

17. Johnson, *Direct Federal Job Creation,* p. 17.

18. "Labor Market Problems of Older Workers," National Council on Employment Policy, Washington, D.C., Spring 1987.

19. Richard V. Burkhauser and Robert H. Haveman, *Disability and Work: The Economics of American Policy* (Baltimore: Johns Hopkins University Press, 1982), p. 74.

7. Linking Welfare with Work

1. Mary Jo Bane and David T. Ellwood, *The Dynamics of Dependence: The Routes to Self-Sufficiency* (Cambridge, Mass.: Urban Systems Research and Engineering, June 1983), pp. 12, 14.

2. U.S. General Accounting Office, *An Evaluation of the 1981 AFDC Changes: Final Report,* (Washington, D.C.: General Accounting Office, July 2, 1985), p. 2.

3. Committee on Ways and Means, U.S. House of Representatives, *Background Material and Data on Programs within the Jurisdiction of the Committee on Ways and Means,* 1986 edition, pp. 405–6.

4. *Smaller Slices of the Pie: The Growing Economic Vulnerability of Poor and Moderate Income Americans,* Center on Budget and Policy Priorities, Washington, D.C., November 1985, p. 30.

5. Robert D. Reischauer, "Welfare Reform and the Working Poor," *Reducing Poverty and Dependence* (Washington, D.C.: Center for National Policy, 1987).

6. U.S. General Accounting Office, *Changes in Rent Burdens and Housing Conditions of Lower Income Households* (Washington, D.C.: General Accounting Office, April 23, 1985), pp. 4, 6.

7. U.S. General Accounting Office, *An Overview of the WIN Program: Its Objectives, Accomplishments, and Problems* (Washington, D.C.: General Accounting Office, June 21, 1982), pp. i–ii.

8. Judith M. Gueron, "Work Initiatives for Welfare Recipients," Manpower Development Research Corporation, New York City, March 1986, p. 5.

9. Bradley R. Schiller, "The Ohio Work Programs: Assessing the First Two Years," prepared for the Ohio Department of Human Services by the Potomac Institute for Economic Research, October 1985, p. 6.

10. Demetra Smith Nightingale, "Federal Employment and Training Policy Changes during the Reagan Administration: State and Local Responses" (Washington, D.C.: Urban Institute, May 1985), p. 81.

11. Gallup Poll, *National Journal,* January 11, 1986, p. 102.

8. Looking Down the Road

1. U.S. Congress, Committee on Ways and Means, *Children in Poverty,* May 22, 1985, p. 409.

2. Congressional Budget Office, *Reducing the Deficit: Spending and Revenue Options,* January 1987, pp. 199, 236, 241.

3. James L. Sundquist, "Has America Lost Its Social Conscience—And How Will It Get It Back?" *Political Science Quarterly,* no. 4, 1986., pp. 517–21.

Index

English, as a second language program (ESL), 72–73
Equal employment opportunity, 8, 11, 66, 77–80, 82, 83
Equal Employment Opportunity Commission, 78, 79, 82, 122
Executive Order 11246, 78, 80

Fair Labor Standards Act, 7, 50, 53, 55, 122. *See also* Minimum wage
Family, rent payments, 105
Federal Adult Education Act, 72–73
Federal minimum wage. *See* Minimum wage
Federal Reserve Board of Governors, and unemployment, 120
Federal taxes. *See* Taxes
Food stamps, 10, 15, 86, 100, 110, 126, 128; coverage and value, 22–23, 102–4, 108; and workfare, 113
Free market economics, 98, 117

Garcia v. San Antonio Metropolitan Transit Authority, 53–54
General Accounting Office: and AFDC, 101, 102; and employment service, 87; WIN study, 111; youths not enrolled in school, 68
Goods-producing industries, 37–38, 67
Greater Avenues for Independence Program (GAIN), 113
Greater Opportunity and Welfare Program (GROW), 113
Griggs v. Duke Power Co., 78–79

Head Start, 9, 71, 81–82, 125
Health insurance, 99, 105, 123, 126–27
House Education and Labor Committee, Labor Standards Subcommittee, 55

Illiteracy, 20, 69–70
Immigrants, 7, 27, 40–41, 44, 70, 73, 119
Immigration and Naturalization Service, 41
Immigration reform act (1986), 41
Income deficit, 22, 27
Income distribution, 16, 119
In-kind benefits 10, 15–16, 22–23, 26, 98–99, 102–6, 110; effect on reducing poverty, 16, 22–23, 105–6. *See also* Food Stamps; Medicaid; Medicare; Public housing assistance
International competition, 6, 36–37, 44, 117

Job Corps, 8, 60, 74–75, 76, 77, 125, 128
Job growth, 38
Job Training Partnership Act (JTPA), 8, 73–74, 85–86, 125
Johnson, Lyndon B., 78

Labor force, 7
Labor market hardship statistics, 30–31
Labor Standards Subcommittee, House Education and Labor Committee, 55
Labor supply, 6
Low-wage job market, 6–7; and immigration, 7, 40–41, 119; and international competition, 6, 36–37, 44; and job trends, 37–39; and minimum wage, 56; and occupational distribution, 28–30; and technological change, 35–36; and unemployment, 30–35, 44; and women and youth, 7, 42–43, 119

Macroeconomic policy, 6, 11, 118, 119, 120
Manpower Development Research Corporation, 112

Sar A. Levitan is research professor and director of the George Washington University Center for Social Policy Studies. Sixteen of his books have been published by Johns Hopkins, including *Programs in Aid of the Poor,* now in its fifth edition. Isaac Shapiro is a senior research analyst at the Center on Budget and Policy Priorities.

Working but Poor: America's Contradiction

Designed by Martha Farlow.
Composed by BG Composition, Inc., in Century Schoolbook.
Printed by R. R. Donnelley & Sons Company on 50-lb. Cream White Sebago.